PRAISE FOR *DO GOOD TO LEAD WELL*

"A very worthy and well-researched read that speaks to both the head and the heart of today's aspiring leader."

—**Doug Conant**

Founder and CEO, ConantLeadership

Former CEO, Campbell Soup Company

New York Times Bestselling Author, TouchPoints

"True leadership is getting people to follow you, not because they have to, but because they want to. In Do Good to Lead Well, *Craig Dowden provides a compelling blueprint to help leaders achieve this most-important goal. My own leadership journey has shown me that being open, vulnerable, and authentic provides a larger return on investment than anything else. Leaders will benefit greatly from the engaging research and concrete tips that are provided in this book."*

—**Jim Whitehurst**

President and CEO, Red Hat

Author, The Open Organization

"A must read for CHROs and CEOs who are grappling with complex decisions and ever-increasing change velocity. Defy the odds of failed change initiatives and unlock the full potential of your people with Craig's evidence-informed approach to positive leadership."

—**Louise Taylor Green**

CEO, Human Resources Professionals Association

"In this must-read book, Craig Dowden provides a clear roadmap for positive leadership. It is the ideal mix of hard science and practical application. As a firm believer in the importance of self-awareness and asking questions, I am happy to see these topics receive substantial coverage. I raise a glass to this timely book and hope you will do the same."

—Frederic Landtmeters

CEO, Molson Coors Canada

"All too often, business leaders feel they must have all of the answers. More often, most are simply afraid to admit their mistakes. In Do Good to Lead Well, Craig Dowden provides a compelling and powerful business case as to why these views are fundamentally misguided. To be at their best, I share the belief that leaders need to be both empathetic and humble, virtues that are appropriately celebrated in this engaging read. Filled with actionable insights, I highly recommend this book to anyone who aspires to lead well."

—W. Brett Wilson

Chairman, Prairie Merchant

Order of Canada Recipient

Bestselling Author, Redefining Success: Still Making Mistakes

"I firmly believe that empowerment is one of the essential ingredients to being a successful CEO, which is why I am such a fan of Do Good to Lead Well. In this book, which is full of compelling research, Craig outlines concrete steps that leaders can follow to get the most out of themselves as well as the people around them. It's an invaluable read for current or aspiring leaders."

—Marsha Smith

President, IKEA Canada

"Combining engaging prose with cutting-edge science, Craig Dowden makes a strong case for why qualities like empathy, self-awareness, civility, and humility underlie great leadership. An essential read for current or aspiring CEOs, managers, and teachers alike."

—David DeSteno

Author, Emotional Success

"Craig Dowden is a wise copilot for your leadership journey. His book on evidence-based, positive leadership, combining insights from interviews conducted with more than fifty CEOs across North America, is a must read for those leaders and managers who want to inspire the best in themselves and in others. The insights in Do Good to Lead Well *are critical not only in the corporate space, but in social impact organizations like Big Brothers Big Sisters. Pick up this book today!"*

—W. Matthew Chater, EdM

President and CEO, Big Brothers Big Sisters of Canada

"Craig Dowden's Do Good to Lead Well *delivers exactly what it promises. It presents hard evidence illustrated with compelling stories, providing a roadmap to anyone committed to the best leadership for our world today. It is destined to become a staple on our 'leadership that makes a difference' bookshelves."*

—Marilee Adams, PhD

Bestselling Author, Change Your Questions, Change Your Life: 12 Powerful Tools for Leadership, Coaching, and Life

Adjunct Professor of Leadership in the School of Public Affairs, American University

"Craig tackles the notion of leadership in a compelling and tangible way, translating the science into everyday practices that can be readily applied to the way we live and work. Through this approach, he shows us that it really is possible to Do Good and Lead Well and his Six Pillars are the roadmap for success. This is a great book on leadership that should be table stakes for every executive."

—Duane Green
President and CEO, Franklin Templeton Canada

"As a serial entrepreneur, I have witnessed firsthand how the quality of leadership can make or break companies. In this engaging book, Craig presents a compelling business case for the tangible benefits of positive leadership and provides useful tips and strategies that readers can put into practice. The insights he shares apply whether you are the founder of a start-up or a seasoned executive of a multinational company. This is essential reading!"

—Eli Fathi
CEO, Mindbridge Ai
Founder/Co-founder of seven companies and
recipient of 2016 Startup Canada Senior Entrepreneur Award

"I enjoy science-based books that cite real research. This is one such book. Dowden's Six Pillars of leadership simplify leadership principles into a useful framework. This book challenges me to be a better leader. I was highly inspired by it."

—Jim Danby
CEO, Danby Appliances

"*I found this book very inspiring. It provides the right mix of theory and practical, real-life examples, which will help and support people who are searching for guidance on how to be an authentic and successful leader.*"

—Stefan Sjöstrand
Commercial Manager, IKEA Group
Former CEO, IKEA Canada

"*I have been fortunate to work with Craig and benefit immensely in my own leadership development from his coaching. In* Do Good to Lead Well, *Craig deftly combines a robust scientific approach and practical, real-world application. It is an incredibly useful blueprint for effectively applying the undeniable power of positive leadership in any organizational context.*"

—Andrew Zimakas
CEO, Sprout Wellness Solutions
Former Head of Corporate Strategy, LoyaltyOne
Former CMO, Tangerine Bank

"*In* Do Good to Lead Well, *Craig Dowden offers valuable insights about how tone starts from the top in any organization and how doing good is the secret to doing well. An important and timely book.*"

—Goldy Hyder
President and CEO, Hill+Knowlton Strategies Canada

"Filled with eye-opening research, Do Good to Lead Well *presents a compelling case that positive leadership is vital—yet sorely lacking—in the modern workplace. Dr. Dowden expertly couples scientific insights with practical application, delivering an actionable, six-step framework for injecting positive leadership into any organization."*

—**Ron Friedman, PhD**
Author, The Best Place to Work: The Art and Science
of Creating an Extraordinary Workplace

"As an introverted CEO who prefers to lead from behind, I often find it difficult to relate to the themes covered in most leadership books. Do Good to Lead Well *was refreshing in that it showcases leadership principles that anyone can benefit from, regardless of their personality or background. It provides a transformative model of positive leadership, which equips executives with the insights and skills they need to thrive, both now and in the future."*

—**Dr. Jack Kitts**
CEO, The Ottawa Hospital

"Craig Dowden deftly dives into the realities of human nature and our relationship with authority to show us how important it is to lead with a moral compass pointed both inward towards our own motivations and outward towards those who trust us to lead them."

—**Matt Wilson**
CEO, BATL

"Even though literature on leadership is abundant, this book was needed. Supported by research and an evidence-based methodology, it defines and illustrates Dowden's Six Pillars of positive leadership in a pragmatic way—at the crossroads of Daniel Goleman's Emotional Intelligence *and Simon Sinek's* Start with Why. *Leaders need to become students of leadership.* Do Good to Lead Well *leverages science to enhance the art of leadership."*

—**André Vincent**

President and CEO, Assumption Life

"Craig Dowden has written an engaging, insightful, and practical book about contemporary views of leadership. It should be required reading for those who aspire to lead with self-awareness, civility, humility, positivity, meaning, and empathy—the organizing rubrics of the book. It should most certainly be read, though most likely will not be by those whose leadership is nasty, brutish, and short tempered.

Dowden has interwoven basic and applied academic research in diverse fields, interviews, exercises and resource material that draw the reader in and excite their curiosity to explore more. It also serves as a thoughtful introduction to contemporary research in positive psychology and organizational behavior and its self-assessment and practical exercises will help leaders in all fields influence and enhance the well-being of those they lead. I expect that even some of the managerial brutes out there will be enlightened and nudged by the deep humanism of this fine book."

—**Brian Little, PhD**

Author, Who Are You, Really? The Surprising Puzzle of Personality *and* Me, Myself *and* Us: The Science of Personality and the Art of Well-Being

"Underpinned by sound research and grounded in coaching sensitivity and experience, Do Good to Lead Well, *is both insightful and practical. Leaders who want to improve their craft should read Craig's book.*

—**Gerry Gaetz**
President and CEO, Payments Canada

"Craig is a trusted authority among today's leaders. With this transformative book, anyone can now readily access his insights on positive leadership and translate them into their everyday practice. I highly recommend this as a guidebook for individuals who are serious about raising their leadership game to the next level."

—**Miro Pavletic**
CEO and Co-Founder, STACK

"In this motivational book, Craig Dowden puts forward a powerful case for effective leadership based on the actual science around "positive leadership." Moving beyond the all-too-common management advice books based on pithy opinions, Craig shows his real skill as an accomplished executive coach and keynote speaker by offering us a compelling and evidentiary guidebook to leadership success through focusing on leading well by leading through a values-based framework. His work should be a mandatory training manual for world leaders!"

—**Michael Garrity**
CEO, Financeit

"In Do Good to Lead Well, *Craig Dowden eloquently delivers a must-read book on leadership and peak performance. The examples and metrics used are so carefully crafted, this book sets the benchmark for excellence! Bravo, Craig!*

—**Samantha Brookes**

CEO, Mortgages of Canada

"I had the privilege of leading a company that scaled very quickly and was eventually acquired by an Accenture- and Microsoft-owned venture. I can say from personal experience that Craig's Six Pillars of positive leadership are critical for success. Do Good to Lead Well *is filled with actionable and real-world insights and provides an invaluable resource for leaders, no matter which environment they are currently operating in. I highly recommend it."*

—**Alim A. Somani**

Executive President, Infusion

DO GOOD TO LEAD WELL

DO GOOD TO LEAD WELL

THE SCIENCE AND PRACTICE OF POSITIVE LEADERSHIP

CRAIG DOWDEN, PhD

ForbesBooks

Published by ForbesBooks, Charleston, South Carolina.
Member of Advantage Media Group.

ForbesBooks is a registered trademark, and the ForbesBooks colophon is a trademark of Forbes Media, LLC.

Printed in the United States of America.

10 9 8 7 6 5 4 3 2 1

ISBN: 978-1-946633-02-6
LCCN: 2018966983

Cover design by Katie Biondo.
Layout design by Megan Elger.

Advantage Media Group is proud to be a part of the Tree Neutral® program. Tree Neutral offsets the number of trees consumed in the production and printing of this book by taking proactive steps such as planting trees in direct proportion to the number of trees used to print books. To learn more about Tree Neutral, please visit **www.treeneutral.com**.

Since 1917, the Forbes mission has remained constant. Global Champions of Entrepreneurial Capitalism. ForbesBooks exists to further that aim by bringing the Stories, Passion, and Knowledge of top thought leaders to the forefront. ForbesBooks brings you The Best in Business. To be considered for publication, please visit **www.forbesbooks.com**.

TABLE OF CONTENTS

ACKNOWLEDGMENTS

This is admittedly the hardest section of the book to write, as I may forget key people and simultaneously not fully capture the impacts those mentioned have had on me.

First and foremost, I want to express my sincere appreciation to my parents. My father was instrumental in showing me the importance of working hard, an ethic which has served me well.

My mom was my earliest role model when it came to positive leadership. She exemplifies each of these pillars and continues to inspire me every day. Thank you for always happily talking with me about my ideas, articles, and multiple versions of this book. Your support and energy are endless. I cannot adequately express how grateful I am for your love and guidance.

I would like to express special thanks to my master's supervisor, Dr. Don Andrews. He was one of the leading internationally recognized experts in the field of forensic psychology, and yet was one of the humblest people I knew. His respect for evidence was profound and shifted the paradigm. He inspired me to be a student of science and take the responsibility to translate research into tangible practice. Although he is no longer with us, I think about him often.

I am also grateful for my doctoral supervisor, Dr. Brian Little. Despite his hectic schedule teaching at both Carleton and Harvard, he continually found time for me and my ideas. His enthusiasm for knowledge about the complexities of the human experience was transformative, as was as his desire to inspire the best in others.

During my professional career, I have had the pleasure of leading multiple consulting teams. In Ottawa, special mentions should be made for JP Michel, Alicia McMullan, Sonia Basili, Rose Matousek, Wayne Pagani, Ingrid Kihl, Peter Frauley, and Louise Lalonde. A very special thanks to Steve Cutler, my other Dad. He was instrumental in living the ideals promoted in this book. His counsel around the importance of doing what's right profoundly affected me. His wisdom, support, and encouragement along the way have been invaluable. In Toronto, special thanks go to Cheddi Suddith, Michael McFadden, Joanna Kraft, and Julie Jonas. I appreciated your enthusiasm for the pillars that are captured in this book.

I would also like to thank all of my clients, especially those who were with me in my earliest days of being an entrepreneur. I have learned so much from working with each of you and look forward to the privilege of collaborating more in the future.

I am grateful for each of the publications with whom I have worked. The Ottawa Business Journal gave me my first "writing gig." Thank you for the opportunity. The *Financial Post* deserves special mention, as they saw the value in offering a column based on the science and practice of positive leadership. They were open to my ideas and supportive of my desire to bring my CEO column to life. Their support opened other doors, including *The Huffington Post*, *Psychology Today*, and *HR Professional*.

I would like to offer deep acknowledgement to Adam Bryant, former *New York Times* columnist and bestselling author of *The Corner Office*. His heartfelt and personal profiles of CEOs inspired me to replicate his column in Canada. Better still, he has been incredibly gracious with his time, providing advice on how to structure my column, despite his demanding schedule. I consider him a mentor.

Which leads me to thank each of the over sixty CEOs I have interviewed over the past four years. Although the list is too big to name individually, I thoroughly enjoyed our conversations, as did the audience. I hope the core principles you promoted are adequately reflected in the pages in this book.

A special thank you goes to W. Brett Wilson, who was my first CEO profile. Despite his presence on the national stage, he personally called me after I wrote a piece about him for the *Ottawa Business Journal*. We have continued a friendship, which I value to this day.

I am grateful to the numerous thought leaders, TED speakers, and bestselling authors who have lent their time and insights to me and my community through interviews, webinars, and podcasts. Thank you (in alphabetical order by last name) Marilee Adams, Robert Biswas-Diener, Susan Cain, Kim Cameron, Doug Conant, David DeSteno, Adam Galinsky, Francesca Gino, Sally Helgesen, Vicki Saunders, Tali Sharot, Barry Schwartz, Ronald Shapiro, Bradley Staats, and Doug Stone.

I met Adam Grant in grad school. He is one of the smartest people I know, and yet his intelligence is only surpassed by his humility. As his presence grew on the international stage, he continued to make time for me and offer advice, recommendations and introductions. His ability to blend research into tangible, valuable practice constantly inspires me. He is the definition of a giver.

I also want to acknowledge Marshall Goldsmith, the world's top-rated executive coach, for his pivotal role in shaping me personally and professionally. I have admired his coaching model, and how he keeps his fee "at-risk," a practice which I follow today. Despite his extraordinary career, impeccable credentials, and heavy demands, he joyously responded to each of my messages. He truly exemplifies his motto "Life is good."

This book would not have been made possible without the support from Advantage|ForbesBooks. Although I cannot acknowledge each of the team members in these pages, I would like to highlight Katherine Beck for her boundless enthusiasm and timely responsiveness. Her attention to detail and desire for excellence brought out the best in me.

A heartfelt thank you to Rusty Shelton, the CEO of Zilker Media, my PR firm, who introduced me to the Advantage|ForbesBooks team.

I cannot thank my editor, Kristin Hackler, enough for her belief in the ideas in this book. Although she came in later on this project, it was made all the better by her involvement. Your influence is felt on these pages.

Two other individuals warrant special mention. My book coach, Lisa Tener, who provided invaluable insight into the book-writing process and helped me flesh out the earliest ideas in this manuscript. James Malinchak, America's Secret Millionaire, has provided wonderful guidance on how to be a professional speaker. I have learned a lot from you. Thank you for sharing your energy and insights.

Last, but not least, several individuals have played a very important role in my entrepreneurial ventures. Thank you to Melissa

Lloyd, Melanie Smith, and Sue Bartholomew. Your belief in the pillars of positive leadership has truly inspired me.

Cara Dowden, thank you for your encouragement to pursue this core project. I appreciated your support as I followed my dreams.

I also appreciate the collaboration and friendship with Andrew Pardy, managing director of Satoruum. I have appreciated all of our work together and your enthusiasm for executive assessment and development.

I am so glad to have met James Baker, CEO of Keynote Group. Your philosophy of delivering maximum value to clients while sharing the science of executive search and development truly resonates with my own. I am excited to launch our new entrepreneurial venture together.

I also promised a shout out to my men's basketball team, Super Club. You model what a great team can accomplish. Thank you for being such an awesome group.

If you have made it to the end, thank you for your thoughtful support to read about the people who have inspired me. I feel like I should end on a random note, which brings a smile to my face every time I read it: keep calm and love pandas! Cheers to that!

FOUNDED IN SCIENTIFIC CURIOSITY

I have always been curious about what makes people tick. Even in high school, I was the person my classmates sought out when they ran into relationship challenges, romantic or otherwise. I listened, asked questions, and explored another way for them to look at things. I was fascinated by how people related to one another, and how that differed so much from person to person, even when faced with the same situation. It made perfect sense that I majored in psychology upon entering university, as I wanted to learn more about the perceptual and emotional elements of human behavior.

As I continued my coursework, I was exposed to industrial-organizational psychology, which immediately resonated with me. Although people have personalities that are fascinating and diverse, organizations also have personalities (i.e., cultures) that are just as complex. I felt that if I combined the two, I would never be bored—there would always be some intriguing aspect of that interplay to dig into.

Fortunately, my hypothesis turned out to be right.

Although I started out pursuing a master's in forensic psychology, I was still fiercely drawn to the interplay between psychology and business. After attending national and international conferences to present my forensic research, I often found myself running out to catch a session on industrial-organizational or consulting psychology. As I became more aware of this field, I was fortunate enough to work with individuals who shared my profound respect for data and the need for evidence-based practices.

My first consulting assignment that was heavily based on organizational psychology was within an IT branch of one of the larger departments within the federal public service of Canada. I worked there as part of a practicum for my PhD, guiding them through a major change initiative. The original assignment went so well that they asked me, along with a handful of other doctoral candidates, to come back and be paid to continue our work. As a "starving student," I was happy to sign on.

One critical piece of feedback that came from our departmental focus groups was the need for upward feedback and more of a focus on leadership development, so I pitched the idea of a 360-degree feedback and coaching program. I emphasized that the evidence-based nature of this approach would be a tremendous value-add, and double as a springboard for conversation with participants.

After receiving approval for the project, I created a 360-degree feedback tool for the department. Several leaders volunteered to participate in this project, from front-line managers all the way up to senior executives. Once the survey was administered and the data were gathered, I sat down with each person and walked through their results. Using their feedback as a foundation, I explored various evidence-based behavioral strategies that they could integrate into their daily leadership practice.

It was an amazing opportunity to pursue my passion early on, and allowed me to see the benefits of these approaches in real time.

These consulting experiences also played an important part after graduation, helping me land the role of managing director of a talent management firm in Ottawa.

I once again had the opportunity to introduce an evidence-based lens to our practice by launching a large-scale survey involving more than three hundred leaders in both Canada and the United States. One of the primary goals of this project was to contribute knowledge to the broader field with our own original data examining the impact of humility on leadership effectivenes[1]. Another was to integrate the findings into our leadership development workshops.

After being recruited for another managing director role for a different firm in Toronto, I was asked to give a presentation at an event for the Conference Board of Canada on the topic of moral leadership. I was delighted to contribute to such a high-profile event. Following my passion, I built an evidence-based business case for why doing the right thing is not just the right thing to do; it is the right thing to do for your organization.

> I built an evidence-based business case for why doing the right thing is not just the right thing to do; it is the right thing to do for your organization.

During my keynote, I had the pleasure of engaging with an audience member who enthusiastically "grilled me," asking a lot of informed questions about the underlying research and how it applied to effective leadership. Afterward, we continued the conversation where I learned that he was an editor with the *Financial Post*, one of Canada's major and most respected national newspapers. He was interested in launching a column, which would be very similar to my approach, written from the perspective of blending science and

---

1   I discuss some of the data on page 93 in Pillar 3–Humility.

leadership practice. He shared that he was personally frustrated by the general lack of evidence-based rigor in other columns and books on leadership, and found my perspective refreshing.

"Would you be interested in writing this type of column?" he asked.

With that, my partnership with *Financial Post Executive* began. It was invigorating to realize that top tier publications were embracing this evidence-based perspective. It also gave me a broader audience with whom I could share all of the latest and greatest research on positive leadership. This led to other opportunities with *The Huffington Post, Psychology Today, HR Professional,* and *The Financial Times.*

One day I was fortunate enough to come across Adam Bryant's *New York Times* column, "The Corner Office." In it, he profiled chief executives, mainly in the US, who shared their lessons learned, their toughest feedback, biggest challenges, and their reasons behind wanting to become a leader. It was very inspiring—so much so that I offered to fly to New York to meet him and he graciously agreed. We spoke about his original inspiration and what he learned in terms of how to share these CEO stories in an authentic way and highlight specific leadership "best practices." This was so powerful for me, not just for the opportunity to learn from Adam, but because it reinforced the importance of not getting so wrapped up in the science that I neglected the practical application of these insights.

It reinforced the importance of not getting so wrapped up in the science that I neglected the practical application of these insights.

As a result of that visit, Adam gave his full blessing for me to bring "The Corner Office" to Canada. I called it "Lessons in Leadership: Insights from Canadian CEOs."

As of this writing, I've interviewed more than sixty CEOs of international organizations, as well as bestselling authors and TED speakers, all of whom have done amazing work in bridging the gap between science and leadership practice. Through this platform, I have been able to share evidence-based insights on leadership with a broad audience. Thanks in large part to that work, I eventually decided to turn my focus to these core passion projects. I continued writing and, four years ago, branched out on my own as an executive coach and keynote speaker, basing my practice on an evidence-informed model of positive leadership.

AN EVIDENCE-BASED ANSWER TO "AIRPORT ADVICE"

What I didn't know when I began this pursuit was how relatively infrequent this kind of approach was in the world of leadership development. In fact, one of the earliest articles I read was called "The Wild West of Executive Coaching" in *Harvard Business Review.*

Despite good intentions, oftentimes the advice that is shared through articles or consulting is derived exclusively from the belief systems of the individual coaches and speakers/trainers. While this can be valuable, it may not correspond to their clients' current reality. What's more troubling, as we shall explore later in this book, is that our ability to recognize the potential gaps in our own behavior and/ or advice is woefully lacking. This sets up a worrisome and potentially damaging situation.

Dr. Kim Cameron, co-founder of the Center for Positive Organizations, calls this "airport advice," because it describes the majority of leadership books that are found on the shelves of airport bookstores. What groups them together, according to Cameron, is that in almost every case these books are based on opinion. "Five Steps" may have resulted in a successful company for one author, or "Seven Buckets" were all someone else needed to become an excellent leader. The suggested courses of action worked for the individual, but there is no guarantee it will be helpful or even applicable to another person's situation.

Daniel Pink's *Drive* was the first book I read that took a different perspective. I loved how he integrated the latest social science into his key messages and delivered this research in an engaging and informative way. Rather than putting out a model of human motivation based on intuition, he took an evidence-based approach by discussing the research and then sharing strategies that readers could use to leverage those insights.

> True coaching is not about being told what to do—it is about discovering the process that works best for that specific leader or organization, integrating the latest research in leadership, team, and organizational excellence into our coaching conversations so we can co-create a set of possible strategies based on the relevant evidence.

Other authors, such as Marshall Goldsmith, Adam Grant, Kim Cameron, and Dan Ariely continue to push this evidence-based approach forward, ensuring that a strong respect for science is integrated into their thinking and what they promote—a perspective that I greatly respect and support in my own work.

I believe that it is far more persuasive when a coach or speaker can say, "Don't take my word for it—here is how this approach worked for half a million people," rather than relying on that coach's personal experience alone. In explaining this philosophy to prospective clients, I often use the analogy of working with them as a co-pilot, rather than as a director. True coaching is not about being told what to do—it is about discovering the process that works best for that specific leader or organization, integrating the latest research in leadership, team, and organizational excellence into our coaching conversations so we can co-create a set of possible strategies based on the relevant evidence.

The other major benefit of an evidence-based approach is that if the science changes, so too would my recommendations. Rather than potentially being blinded by my own biases or beliefs, I provide what the research suggests is the best path forward. My primary concern is to share the most recent findings from the art and science of positive leadership so that my clients can incorporate these insights into their day-to-day practice for their own benefit, as well as for the benefit of the people around them.

The culmination of my journey led me to write this book. Before I discuss the six evidence-based pillars of positive leadership, let's start with an important question: How did we get here?

PILLAR 0

ZERO-SUM, STATUS QUO LEADERSHIP

The road to hell is paved with good intentions.

—Proverb

Despite our best intentions, good leadership is surprisingly rare. As psychologists Robert and Joyce Hogan, creators of the Hogan Assessment, argue, anywhere from 50 to 75 percent of managers either derail or significantly underperform[2].

"How leaders view themselves is largely their own theory about their performance," writes Robert Hogan, "a theory that is rarely

---

2   Joyce Hogan, Robert Hogan, and Robert B. Kaiser, "Management Derailment," American Psychological Association Handbook of Industrial and Organizational Psychology, 2010, https://www.researchgate.net/profile/Robert_Kaiser5/publication/292717475_Management_derailment_Personality_assessment_and_mitigation/links/589b0fb0a6fdcc32dbe24711/Management-derailment-Personality-assessment-and-mitigation.pdf.

tested or evaluated, and is sometimes shockingly out of touch with reality[3]."

It is this out-of-touch view of reality that impairs leaders' decision-making processes and, consequently, leads to complications such as a lack of integrity, poor treatment of employees, and unethical behavior. This misperception is particularly unsettling as we are all highly capable of tricking ourselves into thinking and feeling that we are doing better than we actually are. Furthermore, our capacity to rationalize our behavior puts us at an even greater risk of sliding down a slippery moral slope.

The Hogans' observations dovetail nicely with research on employee engagement conducted by the Gallup organization, a global performance-management consulting company. Although a lot of attention is focused on the relatively low number of actively engaged employees, an equally powerful, if not more troubling statistic, relates to individuals who are considered actively disengaged, which is roughly one-third of employees. According to Gallup, "actively disengaged employees aren't just unhappy at work; they're busy acting out their unhappiness. Every day, these workers undermine what their engaged coworkers accomplish[4]."

Gallup has suggested that active disengagement costs US employers an estimated $450 billion to $550 billion each year in lost productivity. Disengaged employees tend to "kill time," or are "checked out" at the office (e.g., actively counting the days to their retirement/next vacation). They also show little or no concern for how well the organization is performing and their entire work days

3   Dave Winsborough and Robert Hogan, "Bad Managers," Hogan, 2014, https://237jzd2nbeeb3ocdpdcjau97-wpengine.netdna-ssl.com/wp-content/uploads/2014/08/Bad_Managers.pdf.
4   S. Sorenson and K. Garman, "How to tackle U.S. employees' stagnating engagement," *Gallup Business Journal*, June 11, 2013.

revolve around their breaks, which they typically extend for as long as possible[5].

Given the important role of executives in bringing out the best in their teams, one can easily see how active disengagement represents a major problem. This leads us to another important question: What causes people to behave badly as leaders?

WOULD THE GOOD SAMARITAN EXIST TODAY? BUSYNESS AND ITS IMPACT ON DECISION-MAKING

The impacts of the ever-increasing demands of modern living have affected us in countless ways, from the quality of our family relationships, to our enjoyment (and frequency) of leisure time, as well as our physical health. In fact, evidence suggests that more than 40 percent of us check our work email while on vacation, while more than 50 percent of us check it before and after work, and even when we are off sick[6].

This increased busyness does not affect us in these domains alone, as the following classic experiment demonstrates. In fact, time pressure can profoundly compromise our moral decision-making.

Although conducted over thirty-five years ago, research by two psychologists provides a compelling (and arguably chilling) perspective on how the most well-intentioned individual can react inappropriately to an ethical situation in the "right" circumstances[7].

---

5   Ibid.
6   "Americans Stay Connected to Work on Weekends, Vacation and Even When Out Sick," American Psychological Association, September 4, 2013, http://www.apa.org/news/press/releases/2013/09/connected-work.aspx.
7   John M. Darley, and C. Daniel Batson, "From Jerusalem to Jericho: A Study of Situational and Dispositional Variables in Helping Behavior," *Journal of Personality and Social Psychology* 27, no. 1 (1973): 100-108, https://greatergood.berkeley.edu/images/uploads/Darley-JersualemJericho.pdf.

The researchers invited a group of students from the Princeton Theological Seminary to fill in a series of questionnaires designed to measure various aspects of their personality and religiosity. Following this task, each participant was instructed to give a three-to-five-minute impromptu talk on their studies and career plans at a nearby building so experimenters could test their capability to think on their feet.

Beforehand, some of the participants were told about the parable of the Good Samaritan and were invited to incorporate this story into their talk if they felt it would be useful.

For those readers who may be unfamiliar with the parable, in this biblical story, a man is robbed, stripped, beaten, and left for dead along the road to Jericho. Shortly thereafter, a priest ventures down the road and, upon seeing the injured man, crosses to the opposite side. Later, another high-ranking religious figure passes by and also avoids acknowledging or helping the man. Finally, a Samaritan (who was seen as lower class and morally inferior at the time) came upon the man and immediately felt compassion for him. He bandaged the wounds, placed the injured victim on his horse, and took him to the nearest inn, where the Samaritan proceeded to pay for food and lodging.

One of the main lessons to be taken from this parable is that individuals who are perceived as morally inferior are capable of compassionate and merciful acts, while those perceived to be morally superior are capable of callous and unsympathetic behavior.

Following the presentation of the parable, the participants were provided with a map so they could locate where their talk was going to take place. Before leaving, the participants were given one of three sets of instructions:

1. **Low-hurry**—Participants were told there was still some time left before their presentation, but they may as well head over.

2. **Intermediate-hurry**—Participants were told the audience was ready for them so they should leave right away.

3. **High-hurry**—Participants were informed they were late and that the audience was expecting them a few minutes ago, so they had better hurry.

What the experimenters were most interested in was the behavior exhibited by the participants during their walk to the adjoining building. As part of the route outlined on the map, each participant had to pass through a tunnel where the experimenters placed a "victim" (an actor) at the end. The victim was sitting slumped over, eyes closed, and not moving. When the participants got closer, the victim "coughed twice and groaned, keeping his head down." The researchers wanted to see whether the participant would stop and help the man and follow the moral example set forth by the Good Samaritan.

Several fascinating observations surfaced from this experiment. First, whether or not the participants were instructed to give a talk on the Good Samaritan had no impact whatsoever on their response to the victim. In other words, even though the individuals were primed to think about the importance of helping others and were about to talk about this very message in front of a large audience, this did not sway them to tend to the needs of the planted victim.

The second, and arguably most important, finding was that time pressure was the only factor that affected the responses. Sixty-three percent of the participants in the low-hurry condition offered help to the victim while 45 percent of people in the intermediate condition responded in this way. The most striking result was that only 10 percent of people in the high-hurry group stopped to help. In fact, the researchers noted "on several occasions, a seminary student going to give his talk on the parable of the Good Samaritan literally *stepped over the victim* as he hurried on his way."

The following is one of the overall conclusions of the authors, which is still remarkably relevant today: "It is difficult not to conclude from this that the frequently cited explanation that ethics becomes a luxury as the speed of our daily lives increases is at least an accurate description".

Application to a Business Context

This study raises several important points for reflection. First, even without the introduction of the parable of the Good Samaritan, it would be reasonable to assume that students in a seminary should be naturally inclined to help someone in need. Although it could be argued that the students were afraid of the victim, this was likely not the case, as it was not raised in any of the debriefing interviews. In fact, the vast majority of the participants mentioned that they had noticed the victim was in need, but still continued on their way. Furthermore, this experiment was conducted on the crowded grounds of Princeton University, which should certainly diminish any perceived threat on the part of the participants.

Why did individuals, who by their very nature should epitomize moral leadership, make an unethical choice? The authors addressed two possible alternatives, both of which are related to business realities that each of us can appreciate:

1. For some of the participants who walked past (or over) the victim, "because of the time pressures, they did not perceive the scene in the alley as an occasion for an ethical decision".

One clear-cut example may be time-pressured leaders who berate team members for falling behind or who scold employees for spending time with their families instead of working overtime to complete a project. With the pressure to meet deadlines weighing on them, these otherwise "good" leaders may walk straight into an ethical minefield without even realizing it.

> With the pressure to meet deadlines weighing on them, these otherwise "good" leaders may walk straight into an ethical minefield without even realizing it.

2. The other reported cause for this ethical slip was that the participants felt they were helping the experimenter by performing the lecture in a timely manner. This created an internal conflict whereby the individual was torn between helping the victim and proceeding to give his or her assigned talk. Given the authority of the researcher over the vague needs of the victim, one can see how personal ethics may be compromised when those in positions of authority make requests of us. In a business context, this study demonstrates how employees may follow the directives of senior leaders even if those directives violate their own morals. History is filled with examples (e.g. Ford Pinto, ENRON, Wells Fargo, to name a few) where the integrity

> In a business context, this study demonstrates how employees may follow the directives of senior leaders even if those directives violate their own morals.

of many individuals was severely compromised in this manner.

"SHOCKING" ETHICAL LAPSES: THE MILGRAM STUDIES

Psychologist Stanley Milgram conducted some of the most widely cited studies in the field of psychology, which demonstrate how situational factors can impede our decision-making.

At the time, Dr. Milgram was fascinated by the atrocities of World War II, specifically, how high-ranking and often good-hearted people could follow the moral bankruptcy imposed by Adolf Hitler. Milgram's widely replicated study has shed light on some of the darker recesses of the human existence.

In his most well-known experiment, Milgram paired two participants, one of whom was naive to the goal of the study (the teacher) and one who was an accomplice (the student).

At the outset, the experimenter explained that the purpose of the study was to explore the relationship between performance and punishment in the context of memory recall. The role of teacher and student would be randomly assigned by asking the participant to pick a folded piece of paper out of a hat. Unbeknownst to the actual participant, both slips of paper were labeled "teacher," which ensured the accomplice would always be the "student."

Once the roles were "assigned," the teacher and student went into adjacent rooms, with the student being strapped into a chair with an electrode attached to his wrist. There was also some paste applied "to avoid blisters and burns."

The teacher was then told what was expected. Specifically, a word pair would be read to the student to test his memory[8]. After a brief pause, the teacher would say one of the words from the pair and provide the student with four alternatives. If the student answered the question correctly, the teacher would proceed to the next question. On the other hand, if the student was incorrect, the teacher would be required to deliver an electric shock as punishment.

The experiment was designed such that the teacher had to increase the intensity of the shock with each wrong answer (there were thirty levels in all, with fifteen-volt increments starting at fifteen volts). This continued up to a level labeled "Danger: Severe Shock" at 420 volts. The last level was labeled XXX and corresponded to voltage levels of 435 and 450. Although there were no actual shocks delivered, the accomplice was coached on the degree to which he should respond to these painful stimuli. This ranged from mild moans/groans to yelps and even screams for help.

To continue the deception, the teacher was administered a forty-five-volt shock by the experimenter (which was painful) so he would have an idea of how the different levels of shock would feel to the student.

At the beginning of the experiment, the student did relatively well in recalling the words correctly. However, by design, as time wore on, the student made more mistakes. As you can imagine, as the level of the shocks climbed higher and the pained expressions of the student intensified, the teachers became increasingly uncomfortable and expressed concern about ending the experiment, or would ask the experimenter whether they should or could stop administering the shocks.

---

8   It should be noted that all of the participants and researchers in this particular experiment were male.

The experimenters were given four different levels of responses to these objections to try and push the teacher to continue. These were: "Please continue," "The experiment requires you to continue," "It is absolutely essential that you continue," and lastly, "You have no other choice. You must go on!"

If the teacher still wished to discontinue following the fourth prompt, the experimenter would end the session. Otherwise, it would proceed until the teacher had administered the maximum shock level three times.

The results of this experiment were chilling and revealed the extent to which individual behavior can be corrupted under the guise of authority. Overall, almost two-thirds (65 percent) of the teachers administered the shock to the maximum intensity (450 volts). What made these findings even more disturbing was the fact that the students were yelling their objections to continuing and in some cases the student informed the teacher at the outset that he had a heart condition. Not surprisingly, Milgram concluded that obedience to authority was a very powerful and potentially destructive human motivator.

> Milgram concluded that obedience to authority was a very powerful and potentially destructive human motivator.

Application to a Business Context

Translating the results of Milgram's experiment into a corporate environment provides some valuable insight into how unethical decisions may be made by well-meaning individuals in the face of authority. In this case, the authority figure is someone with considerable control over their employees' career paths and ultimately their quality of life (both inside and outside the organization, if things such as promotions and benefits are unfairly given or withheld). Clearly, this can cause extreme pressure to follow orders.

While you may think you would act differently if you were in the experiment, additional research conducted by Milgram seriously questions this assumption. When he surveyed a group of students before the experiment occurred and asked them to predict what percentage of participants would administer the most severe shock possible to the students, on average, people felt only 1.2 percent of the teachers would do so (with the range being 0-3 percent). Considering that the actual result was 65 percent, this, in itself, is remarkable.

If two-thirds of Milgram's participants shocked people to the highest levels within the confines of a voluntary and artificial laboratory because of the prompts of an experimenter whom they just met, what is the percentage of people who may act unethically in a business environment, where more is at stake?

THE "PLASTIC CASH" EFFECT

When it comes to cheating, people tend to do it predictably based on what Dan Ariely, professor of behavioral economics at Duke and MIT, calls a "fudge factor."

"We have a goal to look in the mirror and feel good about ourselves," said Ariely in an interview with *Wired* magazine, "and we have a goal to cheat and benefit from cheating. And we find that there's a balance between these two goals. That is, we cheat up to the level that we would find it comfortable [to still feel good about ourselves][9]."

---

9   Kim Zetter, "TED: Dan Ariely on Why We Cheat," *Wired*, June 28, 2018, https://www.wired.com/2009/02/ted-1/.

Ariely has tested this fudge factor a number of ways, from telling test subjects to pay themselves for each correct answer on an unchecked math test, to leaving sodas in dorm room refrigerators to see if anyone would take drinks that obviously did not belong to them.

Interestingly, his research uncovered that, while people would take cans of soda, they would never take the dollar bills that were left out in the open on plates in the same dorm break rooms, even though the monetary value was the same.

The difference, Ariely explained, was the distancing effect created by the object as opposed to the actual cash. Taking a dollar bill feels like stealing, but we can often justify taking someone else's soda, reasoning that they may have left it for us on purpose, or because someone once stole one of our sodas, taking this one is justified.

To further test his "distancing theory," Ariely conducted another experiment—asking students to pay themselves for each correct answer on a math test that no one checked—using plastic tokens instead of cash to see if it would increase the amount of cheating ... and it did.

"As we deal with things that are more distant [from] money, the easier it is to cheat and not think of yourself as a bad person." He suggests this tendency is especially concerning considering how quickly our society is moving away from cash. It is far easier for executives, he explains, to backdate stock options when they do not think of those options as cash.

This means that leaders and business executives must remain acutely aware of how these factors influence our capacity to make moral choices.

HOW "DISTANCING" IMPACTS MORAL DECISION-MAKING

Milgram and his colleagues also explored the role of distancing in their future experiments. Although not as well-known as the initial research, Milgram and others conducted several replication studies, each with its own unique twist on his original design, which provided powerful, if not equally relevant, observations about human nature.

In one such experiment, Milgram examined how the level of compliance of the student was affected by their proximity to the teacher. To do this, he recruited another individual to be involved. In this case, the third participant was only responsible for administering the memory test while the teacher and learner followed the original design. Milgram was interested to know whether creating an extra layer between the teacher and the student (e.g., because there was no need to administer the shock, just administer the test that would potentially lead to it) would change their behaviors.

Under these conditions, 93 percent of the participants continued to perform the memory test until the student was shocked to the highest level. This is extraordinary, as it suggests that by simply removing their finger from the button, it changed the participants' outlook and sense of responsibility for the whole situation.

In another fascinating twist, Milgram upped the ante for the teachers. Although most people cringe at what came next, in future trials, the teacher was seated in the same room as the student. Rather than being separated from what was going on by being across the hall, the teacher had a front row seat to what was happening. Not surprisingly, compliance with the experimenter's wishes to continue went down, with 40 percent agreeing to deliver shocks to the student at the highest level. Other trials necessitated that the teacher place the student's hand on the device that was transferring the shock. This resulted in the lowest level of compliance: 30 percent, which was less than half of what occurred under the original design.

Although some may be amazed at the still-high level of compliance, it raises a very interesting perspective regarding our capacity to engage in immoral acts based on the context. Although rationally the participants knew that their actions were leading to the shocks when they were in another room, as they heard the screams and cries for help as a result, witnessing the consequences of their deeds in person changed their behavior in profound ways.

Application to a Business Context

Stepping back once again and applying this experiment within a corporate environment provides disturbing, yet compelling, insight into what forces allow leaders to engage in such thoughtless and careless actions.

Senior executives can have a hard time seeing or feeling the consequences of their actions because they are so far removed from the front line. The "facts" that they work with are objective data, including profitability, headcount, etc. There are no names, no faces, attached to their actions.

The perilous impacts of psychological distancing are amplified by corporate wordsmithing, with phrases such as downsizing, restructuring, or even "right-sizing" employed to make these actions seem more palatable. Terms such as firings or terminations are often avoided at all costs. When presented this way, there may be little wonder that senior executives may not truly appreciate that they may be handling these scenarios callously and thoughtlessly.

While I am not condoning how some executives carry out these decisions, I am suggesting that it is important for each of us to recognize that we could easily act out of character in a similar way if we do not pause and think about how our context may be short-circuiting our moral compass.

WE DON'T SEE THINGS AS *THEY* ARE. WE SEE THEM AS *WE* ARE

Another psychological pitfall that can hamper our ability to lead well is the "false consensus effect," which is the erroneous belief that most people are "like us."

To investigate this phenomenon, Stanford University Professor Lee Ross set up several intriguing experiments. In the first study, participants were asked to read about an unresolved conflict. Afterwards, the participants were given two possible alternatives to resolve it. Then, they were asked three questions:

- What option do you think other people will believe is best?

- What option do you think is best?

- Can you describe the types of people who would pick choice number one and choice number two?

As you may have predicted, the majority of participants thought that other people would pick the same choice they did. This was true, no matter which of the two choices they selected.

Not surprisingly, participants also had wildly opposing views concerning the types of people who would make these choices.

When describing people who would be prone to select the other choice, much more negativity was attributed to their personalities and motives, with some even positing that there must be "something wrong" with them.

Ross and his team replicated this effect in another study where participants were asked whether they would be willing to wear signs that read "Eat at Joe's" and march around campus for thirty minutes. Once again, students who agreed to wear the sign felt that significantly more people would do the same (e.g., 62 percent thought other people would say "yes"). In the refusal group, however, only 33 percent of them felt other people would wear the sign.

Application To A Business Context

The erroneous belief that the majority of people think the same way we do can be seen in how leaders celebrate the accomplishments of their team members. Specifically, research suggests leaders typically reward their employees in the same way in which the leaders prefer to be rewarded[10].

If a manager loves being brought up on stage and cheered for an accomplishment, he or she may likely want to do the same thing for all of their team members. However, not everyone appreciates or desires this kind of recognition. Some may even be terrified of it.

The key takeaway here is that leaders need to acknowledge that not everyone enjoys the same things they do. In fact, the majority of people likely do not share the same perspective. Instead of assuming, the best leaders ask first, then reward.

---

10   This insight is attributed to research conducted for the Hogan Motives, Values, and Preferences Inventory, a widely used assessment tool.

THE PERILS OF CONFORMITY

Imagine you are asked to participate in a study on visual perception. When you arrive, the experimenter welcomes you and points out your seat, which is to her left at the front of the table. She explains that she will hold up three lines of varying heights in one hand and a single line in the other. Your job is to tell her which of the three lines correspond to the single line.

Starting with the person immediately across from you, the experimenter asks each participant for an answer. Everyone, including you, sees that the answer is "A" and respond accordingly. The experimenter then holds up another set of three lines and a single line, and asks the same question. Again, everyone in the room gives the right answer.

On the third round, you immediately see that the answer is again "A," and wait your turn. However, as each participant gives an answer, they all reply "C."

Scratching your head, squinting your eyes, and searching for some sort of visual aid, you try to figure out what you must be missing. The answer is clearly "A" but apparently you are the only one who thinks so. Then it is your turn: "Which of the three lines is the correct match?"

What do you think you would say?

In questioning ourselves, even though we are certain of the correct answer, psychologist Solomon Asch famously demonstrated our innate and overpowering urge to belong. In his research, he found that 75 percent of participants conformed to the group answer at least once.

Application to a Business Context

How many times have we been in meetings where there is unanimous agreement on the outside, yet we may feel tremendous turmoil and resistance on the inside?

In his book *Leading With Questions*, Dr. Michael Marquardt highlights several major historical disasters, such as the Bay of Pigs invasion, the Challenger, as well as the Titanic, where smart and well-meaning people failed to speak up because of the influence of the majority. In their minds, since no one else was questioning the decisions that were being made, they thought they must have been missing something. Afraid of being seen as stupid or ostracized by the group, they stayed silent. When reflecting on these events, these individuals talked about the profound regret they felt for not standing up for the truth in that critical moment.

THE CORE RESPONSIBILITY OF LEADERSHIP

One of our most significant challenges as leaders is learning to accept that we are flawed, that we can be influenced, and that we have to step outside of ourselves if we are going to understand how our decisions impact and influence others; and in understanding this, taking the necessary steps to change.

I regularly meet with executives who face an almost existential crisis when it comes to reconciling their desire to succeed with perceived conflicts with their own moral compass. Time and again, these initial conversations come back to the leader's belief that one can be very nice and values-driven, or they can be successful; that they can either do good *or* they can lead well.

Yet in all of the research I've read and personally conducted, this belief could not be further from the truth. Great leaders are not brash, callous giants that stomp on those who get in their way and motivate their team from a place of fear. Rather, they do good *and* lead well.

As leaders, we not only have the responsibility to encourage positive behavior in our teams, we also have to exemplify it. We could easily say that we believe our employees are our most important resource, yet if our actions say, "Make money by any means possible because at the end of the day, you are your metrics," then what are your employees most likely to focus on?

This potential misalignment poses a significant threat to leadership and organizational success. As former *New York Times* "Corner Office" columnist Adam Bryant pointed out to me, "If you want to kill company morale, the best way to do it is to print your core values out, post them on a wall, and then contravene them at every opportunity." Being a great leader is not about what you say or what you aspire to do—it is about who you are and how you lead.

> Being a great leader is not about what you say or what you aspire to do—it is about who you are and how you lead.

THE SIX PILLARS OF POSITIVE LEADERSHIP

Developing positive leaders and maximizing employee engagement is of paramount concern to organizations today. If you conduct a Google search on this topic, you can get anywhere from 15 to 20 million entries. Countless models exist, which suggest different ways to accomplish this important goal. This leaves leaders and organizations wondering how to do the right thing to obtain the desired result.

This book summarizes the social, behavioral, and management sciences to present six evidence-informed pillars of positive leadership. Substantial, independent research has demonstrated that leaders who follow these six evidence-informed pillars accrue significant tangible and intangible benefits, ranging from increased employee engagement to more innovation and higher revenue. In the following pages, we will explore how the "softer side" of leadership maximizes our individual and collective success.

Whether leading a small team, large division, or an entire organization, these evidence-informed pillars provide a roadmap on how to transform your workplace, and challenge you to leverage the power of doing good to lead well.

Pillar 1: Self-Awareness

Self-awareness plays a critical role in leading well, as it is only through knowing who we are and how we come across to others that we can capitalize on our strengths, identify our weaknesses, manage our blind spots, and take appropriate action accordingly.

Every time we speak or act, we judge ourselves based on our *intentions*. However, because other people do not know what we're thinking or feeling, they assess our words and behaviors based on their *impact*. For example, when we make a comment intended to be light-hearted, someone else may hear it as derogatory.

These moments provide golden opportunities to grow our self-awareness and learn why something we did, or said, did not have the impact we intended. Yet we rarely take advantage of these potential learning experiences. Instead, we are more likely to try and explain ourselves, placing the blame on the other person for misunderstanding us, or the situation.

For this reason, as well as many others that we will discuss, self-awareness is the cornerstone of positive leadership.

Pillar 2: Civility

No matter where we sit in an organization, we look up to understand how to behave. This is particularly important for high-potential employees who aspire to positions of leadership. They need to know how to get ahead, and if they see the current leadership exhibiting disrespectful, toxic behaviors, that is what they are going to emulate. In the same vein, when team members are treated with disrespect, they are less likely to put forth their best efforts, or even care about the success of the organization. In this way, incivility can create a self-perpetuating downward spiral of negativity that can become challenging, if not impossible, for an organization to recover from.

Civility may be defined as "politeness and courtesy in behavior and speech," yet it is far less formal than this explanation implies. Civility is a necessary ingredient of growth and success, regardless of whether you are an organization or a human being. Without it, failure is inevitable.

Pillar 3: Humility

When people are asked to rate the most important qualities that a leader should possess, humility is often close to, if not dead, last. Unfortunately, the perception is that humility makes you seem weak. And yet, when people are asked how they feel about a leader who exhibits humility (e.g. by genuinely apologizing for a behavior), they rarely say that they perceive that leader as "weak." Instead, they almost instantly have a greater respect for that leader and admire them for their courage and strength of character.

Humility is being aware of our strengths while simultaneously recognizing that we do not have all the answers, and that we are willing to ask others for their knowledge and perspective. Being humble allows us to take full advantage of the insights available to us in our surrounding environment.

Although humility may seem counterintuitive, it is the very act that inspires confidence in others about our capacity to lead well.

Pillar 4: Focus on the Positive

In focusing on the positive, we are not ignoring the negative. Instead, we are giving our energy and attention to those things that engender positivity.

When we are in a positive frame of mind, research suggests we interact with our environment more effectively, as we look for opportunities to "broaden and build" our perspective[11]. When we are in a negative frame of mind, however, we contract from that openness and want to avoid risk: we become much more protective and cautious in orientation. In business, this can mean the difference between an organization's survival or failure. In looking toward the future with a positive frame of mind, a company is more likely to be innovative and challenge the status quo. When this outlook is replaced by fear, however, organizations are more likely to shut themselves off, avoid risks, and embrace the mind-set of simply staying the course. As we shall see, without a positive focus, organizations are doomed to fail.

---

11   See more on positive psychologist Barbara L. Fredrickson's "broaden and build" theory in pillar 4: Focus on the Positive.

Pillar 5: Meaning and Purpose

Based on global surveys, the most important driver of employee engagement is "the opportunity to do meaningful work[12]." Essentially, this means making a contribution to something above and beyond ourselves. If team members believe that their work is pointless, they quickly lose enthusiasm and eventually leave. Yet meaning and purpose can be found in every job—it is a primary responsibility of the leader to ensure that every team member knows where to find it. When employees are dedicated to the purpose of what they do, not only does it drive better results, it also improves retention. The opportunity to make a difference is an invaluable currency.

Pillar 6: Empathy

Empathy has been identified as the most important skill to develop by many of the leading experts and organizations today because it generates a level of interpersonal understanding and acceptance that we, as humans, crave. Empathy allows us to step outside of ourselves and not only see situations through another's eyes, but to understand things from their point of view.

Empathy is also a powerful competitive advantage to foster within organizations, as it is a quality that is steadily declining. According to University of Michigan researcher Sarah Konrath, "College kids today are about 40 percent lower in empathy than their counterparts of twenty or thirty years ago[13]." In a related but separate study, she

---

12 Paul Fairlie, "Meaningful Work, Employee Engagement, and Other Key Employee Outcomes," *Philosophy of the Social Sciences* 13, no. 4 (December 6, 2011): 508-25, http://journals.sagepub.com/doi/abs/10.1177/1523422311431679?journalCode=adha.

13 Diane Swanbrow, "Empathy: College Students Don't Have as Much as They Used to," University of Michigan News, May 27, 2010, http://ns.umich.edu/new/releases/7724-empathy-college-students-don-t-have-as-much-as-they-used-to.

and her fellow researchers found a similar decline in kindness and helpfulness across a nationally represented sample of Americans.

As biologist and professor of psychology, Frans de Waal notes in his book *The Age of Empathy: Nature's Lessons for a Kinder Society*, life is not simply a perpetual struggle to survive—we *depend* on each other to survive. Nature is full of examples of cooperation and empathy, and we would not be here today without these qualities.

"Human morality," de Waal writes, "is unthinkable without empathy."

DO GOOD TO LEAD WELL

The preceding Six Pillars may seem to be outside of the bounds of normal business—that they can get in the way of making the "tough decisions" that are in the "best interest for the company"—yet when we sit down and speak about leadership today, we learn that these pillars are exactly what people are yearning for. We want leaders who are humble and willing to admit that they do not have all the answers. We want leaders who take the time to see things from another perspective.

This book is for executives, leaders, and aspiring leaders who want to challenge the status quo of leadership; people who want to raise their game and have a transformative impact on themselves and the people around them.

The goal is for you to understand on the deepest level that effective leadership is not a choice between doing the right thing or being successful. It's about setting the example, and doing good to lead well.

PILLAR 1

SELF-AWARENESS

*At the center of your being you have the answer; you
know who you are and you know what you want.*

—Lao Tzu

As a leader, Susan had great intentions. She was highly committed to supporting the aspirations of each of her team members and wanted those who were interested to emulate her path to take on more responsibility. She had experienced tremendous success in her career thus far and wanted to pay it forward.

To facilitate her growth, Susan chose to undertake a 360-degree feedback exercise, which involved collecting feedback from her direct reports, peers, and supervisors. She received terrific scores on a lot of questions—people saw her as warm, approachable, and concerned for their well-being. What was most interesting was that her number one area for development turned out to be her tendency to micromanage.

Susan was devastated by this result. In her mind, there was no label worse than "micromanager"; it was the pinnacle of poor leadership.

"How do these results make sense?" she asked, sounding exasperated. "How can I be seen as warm and approachable while also scoring high on micromanagement?"

As her coach, I asked her not to judge the feedback at this moment. Instead, our job was to explore and make sense of it. To do this, I suggested an exercise.

"If I were a member of your team, walk me through how you would manage me on a regular basis. What's your style?" I asked.

Susan explained that she would come over to my desk first thing in the morning and ask about my to-do list and how I planned to tackle it for the day. Then, after mid-morning coffee break, she would drop by to see how things were going. She would conduct one final check-in during the mid-afternoon and followed this exact cycle each and every day.

She was quite proud of her approach because it was one she picked up from a former boss. In fact, she believed that she was in her current role thanks to his influence. And since she had experienced so much success, she wanted to give her staff the same "benefits" she experienced.

"That makes sense," I said. "So my next question is: 'Have you ever explicitly talked with your team about why you engage in these behaviors?'"

"No," she replied.

"Okay," I said. "Recognizing that you haven't explicitly explained your behaviors, what do you think the average person would conclude if they were exposed to this management style without any context?"

She leaned back in her chair.

"Oh my god, I'm a micromanager."

This was a massive "aha!" moment for Susan as she suddenly understood how she had lost some key people due to this approach. She had also mistakenly assumed that since she was so warm and friendly, people would openly talk with her if they had any concerns. It was a painful and powerful lesson.

DEFINING SELF-AWARENESS

"Do you have an accurate sense of who you are and how other people perceive you?" This question is fundamentally at the core of self-awareness.

Most of us assume that our motivations are clear to the people around us. In Susan's case, she wanted her team members to succeed and felt that her constant checking in would be viewed as supportive. She never considered how her behaviors could be construed as micromanaging, especially since she was innately a caring and compassionate individual.

This kind of disconnect can quickly lead to frustration, with leaders wondering, "How could my employees possibly think this is who I am as a leader? What's wrong with them?"

These gaps, also called "blind spots," are universal, which is why increasing our level of self-awareness may be one of the most important steps we can take to maximize our effectiveness. The more we are aware of who we are and how we come across to others, the more capable we are in navigating the different situations and personalities that we encounter at work and in life.

THE SCIENCE OF SELF-AWARE LEADERSHIP

The Science of Self-Aware Leadership

1. Improved Financial Performance

2. Higher Levels of Personal and Professional Success

3. Greater Job Fit and Organizational Success

Self-awareness provides a critical leadership advantage, and there is considerable empirical evidence supporting its benefits.

1. Improved Financial Performance

In investigating the potential financial benefits of self-awareness, Ginka Toegel and Jean-Louis Barsoux, professors of organizational behavior and leadership at IMD in Lausanne, Switzerland, surveyed members of the Stanford Graduate School Business Advisory Council, asking, among other things, "What skills are the most important for your MBA students to learn?" The prevailing response was "self-awareness."

"Executives need to know where their natural inclinations lie in order to boost them or compensate for them," the authors explained[14]. "Self-awareness is about identifying personal idiosyncrasies—the characteristics that executives take to be the norm, but actually represent the exception."

Similarly, Korn Ferry found a correlation between a company's financial performance and the level of self-awareness of its executive team. In their report "A Better Return on Self-Awareness," researchers

---

14   Leslie Brokaw, "Self-Awareness: A Key to Better Leadership," *MIT Sloan Management Review*, May 7, 2012, https://sloanreview.mit.edu/article/self-awareness-a-key-to-better-leadership/.

analyzed close to 7,000 self-assessments from executives employed at publicly traded organizations, starting with a closer look into their blind spots—the difference between an individual's self-assessment and how others perceived them[15]. The poorest performing companies had leaders with 20 percent more blind spots than those at more financially successful organizations.

Additionally, leaders at the poorest performing companies were 79 percent more likely to have lower overall self-awareness than those organizations with a much stronger financial performance.

The authors argue that one of the primary reasons why self-awareness is so valuable is that it allows individuals to make better professional and personal choices. However, despite its importance, the findings indicate "self-awareness is generally in short supply."

2. Higher Levels of Personal and Professional Success

There is a common belief that certain personality profiles are more likely to succeed. To test this hypothesis, Dr. Travis Bradberry used the DiSC—an assessment tool based on four behavioral traits: dominance, inducement, submission, and compliance—to look at fourteen different personality profiles and examine any potential links to personal and professional success. As he outlines in his book *Self-Awareness: The Hidden Driver of Success and Satisfaction*, his research uncovered no special profile that separates successful from unsuccessful people. In fact, success was equally spread out across each of the fourteen personality types. Instead, after reviewing more than half a million assessments, his research showed that the most

15   David Zes, "A Better Return on Self-Awareness," Korn Ferry Institute, August 9, 2013, https://www.kornferry.com/institute/647-a-better-return-on-self-awareness.

important driver for success was not the personality profile of the individual, but rather his or her level of self-awareness.

His research echoed the work done by Korn Ferry, as Dr. Bradberry also reported that self-awareness was comparatively rare; only 29 percent of his sample possessed a reasonable level of self-awareness. Another fascinating and revealing discovery was that more than 70 percent of respondents experienced "considerable difficulty managing the stress and interpersonal conflict that are fostered by low self-awareness." When he focused his analyses on the workplace, he discovered that 83 percent of top performers were high in self-awareness while only 2 percent of the worst performers were highly self-aware[16].

The above research collectively reached the same conclusion as Susan, who was profiled earlier in this chapter—people with a high level of self-awareness are less likely to stumble into conflict or run into other challenges because of their blind spots.

3. Greater Job Fit and Organizational Success

A study conducted by Green Peak Partners and Cornell University that involved almost 100 senior level executives (half of which occupied the C-suite) began with a simple question: "What factors predict executive success[17]?" Their results revealed that self-awareness is a critical, if not the most important, component. What's more, this conclusion applied across all sectors, industries, and company sizes.

How does self-awareness play a role in a company's overall success? The answer may lie in provocative research conducted by Boris Groysberg, Andrew McLean, and Nitin Nohria, which revealed

---

16   Travis Bradberry, *Self-awareness: The Hidden Driver of Success and Satisfaction* (New York, NY: Penguin Group, 2009), 35.
17   "New Study Shows Nice Guys Finish First," American Management Association. http://www.amanet.org/training/articles/new-study-shows-nice-guys-finish-first. aspx.

that despite an impressive pedigree and experience, not all executives are equally portable[18].

Groysberg and colleagues focused on twenty Harvard alumni who were employed at General Electric and who were then poached by other companies. Initially, their analyses revealed that the market value of the hiring company spiked when the former GE employees came on board. However, over the next three years, only about half of those hires ended up creating value for their new companies while the other half significantly diminished it.

The reason turned out to be job compatibility. The alumni who were more self-aware and understood the type of environment in which they worked best were more likely to select an opportunity that was best suited to their approach and strengths, which translated into a more successful engagement for everyone. Those leaders who were low in self-awareness did not possess this insight, and blindly believed that they could replicate their success in any environment. As scientific and anecdotal research shows, if there is a partial or poor match between the individual executive and his or her employer, they are more likely to become frustrated and either walk out the door, or be shown to it.

BE AWARE OF THE SELF-SERVING BIAS

The vast majority of people have a positive self-view. We want to see ourselves in the best possible light, yet that desire often comes at the cost of blaming others for what may actually be our own fault. This faulty perception is a critical component of the self-serving bias.

18   Boris Groysberg et al., "Are Leaders Portable?" *Harvard Business Review*, August 1, 2014, https://hbr.org/2006/05/are-leaders-portable.

For example, how often do you jump out of bed in the morning thinking, "I cannot wait to systematically undermine my own success today?" I doubt very often. Instead, we believe that we have a solid handle on what we are doing and where we are going.

This is all well and good, of course. We need to feel as though we are prepared to tackle our day, to take on the next big challenge and overcome the odds. Where the difficulty occurs is when this positive self-view begins to cloud our judgement when it comes to our sense of self.

When speaking with audiences, one of my favorite pieces of research I like to mention happened in the mid-1990s where *US News and World Report* surveyed several thousand of its readers, asking them the following question: "How likely is it that each of the following celebrities will get into Heaven?" The scale went from "Not at all likely" to "Very likely." The list included era-specific icons such as Bill Clinton, Michael Jordan, Princess Diana, and Michael Jackson.

While the top scoring celebrity on the list—Mother Teresa—is not surprising to people; they are taken aback when they learn that only 79 percent of survey respondents felt that she was "Likely" or "Very likely" to get into Heaven.

What made this finding even more compelling was when the readers were asked to rate how likely they themselves were to get into Heaven. Strikingly, 87 percent stated that they were "Likely" or "Very likely" to get past the pearly gates.

How is it that we feel more deserving of getting into Heaven than Mother Teresa?

This illusory sense of superiority is rooted in the Dunning-Kruger effect; a cognitive bias wherein the vast majority of us rate ourselves as above average in our own abilities, even though this is a statistical impossibility[19]. One of the greatest consequences of holding on to this worldview is that it profoundly hinders our ability to receive and act on feedback in areas where we need to hear it most.

Stephen Covey, world-renowned author of *The Seven Habits of Highly Effective People*, dug into his 360-degree feedback data to find out where people received the lowest scores[20].

Covey's analysis of the seventy-two questions in his survey revealed that people struggled the most in areas related to feedback, with the two lowest scoring items being "Receives negative feedback without becoming defensive," and "Seeks feedback on ways to improve." What was most interesting about this research was that when participants rated themselves in these areas, both items frequently appeared as qualities in which they believed they excelled, often showing up in their top ten.

---

19 This is named after the two researchers, David Dunning and Justin Kruger, who initially discovered this phenomenon.

20 Remember that 360-feedback processes involve a leader receiving feedback from his or her direct reports, peers, supervisor(s), and (sometimes) stakeholders. The best 360-feedback surveys include self-ratings which maximize the potential to raise self-awareness

The blind spot highlighted by Covey's work presents two critical challenges for our development and ultimate success.

First, since we feel that we receive critical feedback so well, we can trick ourselves into believing that people will voluntarily share this type of information if they think we need to hear it. No negative feedback? Then we must be doing a great job.

Secondly, since we believe that we routinely seek constructive feedback on ways that we can improve, we already feel that we are doing it enough. This means that we rarely, if ever, ask people for their impressions of us. However, most people will only offer up that type of information if they feel we are interested in hearing it.

Together, this can create a feedback vacuum wherein we mistakenly assume that people would tell us if we are doing something wrong, because we believe that we are constantly asking for feedback and are highly skilled in receiving it.

The Impact of Self-Serving Bias on Decision-Making Skills

In the workplace, the self-serving bias can significantly impact our quality of decision-making. In their book *Egonomics: What Makes Ego Our Greatest Asset (or Most Expensive Liability)*, authors David Marcum and Steven Smith discuss the results of a survey where they asked almost 2,000 of their clients, "How confident are you in your capacity to make good decisions?" They found that 83 percent of people were either "Confident" or "Very confident" in their own abilities. When they were asked a slightly different question: "How confident are you in the ability of your closest colleagues to make good decisions?, remarkably, only 27 percent of respondents said "Confident" or "Very confident."

Are we that good and is everyone else around us that incompetent?" According to us, the answer is a definitive "Yes!" This is a troubling statistic, as research strongly suggests that diversity drives higher quality decision-making, as well as higher engagement and bottom line results. By holding this misguided perspective, we not only undermine our own success, we also undermine the success of the people around us.

PRACTICING SELF-AWARE LEADERSHIP

Practicing Self-Aware Leadership

1. Conduct a Personality Assessment

2. Engage in a 360-Degree Feedback Assessment

3. Improve How We Deliver Feedback

4. Know Why We Sometimes Act Out of Character and What to Do About It

5. Take Time for Self-Reflection

6. Ask for Informal Feedback

Given its importance to leadership success, how can we become more self-aware?

1. Conduct a Personality Assessment

A personality assessment, also known as a psychometric test, involves the administration of a set of scientifically supported and validated questions carefully constructed to examine our tendencies, style, interpersonal preferences, strengths, and developmental requirements. It essentially provides insight into how we show up in the world, how we communicate, and how other people may perceive us.

This incredibly valuable information provides a baseline from which to gauge where we stand on a variety of traits compared to a population of hundreds of thousands, if not millions, of our peers. For example, when compared to the average person, how assertive are we? What is our proneness to anger, openness to experience, or level of conscientiousness?

RELIABILITY AND VALIDITY: KEY CRITERIA FOR EFFECTIVE ASSESSMENTS

There are two key criteria that separate effective from ineffective assessments: reliability and validity.

Reliability: One of the most important aspects of reliability relates to the stability of the results. If you take the same assessment next month, for instance, will the findings be consistent? If an inventory provides inconsistent results across each application over time, it is unhelpful and potentially dangerous to inform hiring decisions because the profile of the individual will not be the same. In other words, what might be seen as a strong candidate during the initial screening process may have an unattractive profile in subsequent administrations.

By the same token, unreliability also renders an inventory relatively useless when it comes to creating a development plan or training program for an employee.

We need consistency in the profile results or else it does not enable leaders to make strategic decisions in how to acquire and develop their talent.

Validity: Although reliability is important, validity is another critical feature. A key indicator of validity involves how well the assessment results predict outcomes of interest to the user, such as job performance or organizational commitment. If the inventory does not exhibit predictive validity or has never been tested as such, organizations and leaders take a strategic risk that while the questions may seem interesting; they are not associated with key performance indicators of interest.

It is important to point out and caution that frequency of use or popularity does not necessarily mean the assessment is effective[21].

---

21   Interestingly enough, perhaps the most widely researched and tested model of personality, which has been validated across the globe, has yet to make significant inroads into the corporate landscape. The Five-Factor Model, also referred to as "The Big Five," consists of: openness to experience, conscientiousness, extroversion, agreeableness, and neuroticism (OCEAN) and is the taxonomy on which the NEO-PI-3 Personality Inventory is based. Readers who are interested in learning more about assessing the Big Five with the NEO-PI-3 are encouraged to read: *McCrae, et al.,* "Cross-cultural assessment of the five-factor model: The revised NEO Personality Inventory," *Journal of Cross-Cultural Psychology 29 (1998): 171–188, doi:10.1177/0022022198291009.*

For example, while the MBTI is widely known in corporate settings, bestselling author and Wharton professor Adam Grant wrote a compelling critique of the science (or lack thereof) surrounding the tool, which created quite a stir[22]. Therefore, the mantra "buyer beware" should be applied when it comes to identifying and utilizing any assessments. Despite their potential for delivering high value, the wrong tool, at best, may not yield any particularly pertinent information and at worst, could potentially undermine decision-making and negatively impact individual and organizational effectiveness.

Scientifically Supported Assessment Tools

1. HOGAN ASSESSMENT[23]

Developed by Drs. Robert and Joyce Hogan over thirty years ago, the Hogan is the first personality assessment tool created exclusively for usage in a professional context. It is one of the most scientifically supported instruments on the market. Unlike many of its counterparts, the Hogan has been investigated by many independent investigators and researchers to test its utility and effectiveness.

The user receives three separate reports: The Hogan Personality Inventory; The Hogan Development Survey; and the Motives, Values, and Preferences Inventory. Popularly referred to as our bright side, dark side, and inside, respectively these comprehensive results provide a veritable 360 of an individual across numerous important domains.

The Hogan Personality Inventory (HPI) assesses "normal" personality and consists of seven primary scales (adjustment, ambition,

---

22   For those readers who are interested in checking out the article, please go to the following URL: https://www.psychologytoday.com/ca/blog/give-and-take/201309/goodbye-mbti-the-fad-won-t-die.

23   To see the full list of Hogan scales and sub-scales, see the appendix. Learn more about Hogan assessments at www.hoganassessments.com.

sociability, interpersonal sensitivity, prudence, inquisitiveness, and learning approach) with more than forty qualifying sub-scales[24].

The Hogan Development Survey (HDS) outlines potential "derailers"—those behavioral tendencies that can trip us up when we become overly stressed or too relaxed in a situation. There are eleven derailers identified in the HDS (such as bold, skeptical, leisurely, and dutiful), along with thirty-three sub-scales[25]. This insight provides warning signs so we can know in advance when we are at risk of going off track and take the appropriate steps to avoid it.

Finally, as its name suggests, the **Motives, Values, and Preferences Inventory (MVPI)**, identifies what gets us out of bed in the morning and the type of environment in which we like to work. It allows us to see "inside" of ourselves to recognize what makes us tick when it comes to our work. There are ten motivational drivers in this inventory (such as recognition, power, affiliation, and security), with five sub-scales[26].

2. TAIS[27]

The Attentional Interpersonal Style assessment, or TAIS, was developed by Dr. Robert Nideffer, one of the world's top psychologists. The tool is supported by more than forty years of research and is the assessment method of choice for the US Navy Seals, numerous professional sports organizations (including the NHL and NBA), and corporations around the world. TAIS provides insight into the four key challenge areas that lead to workplace derailment—lack of coachability, low levels of emotional intelligence, lack of motivation,

---

24   See the appendix for the full list of HPI scales and sub-scales.
25   See the appendix for the full list of HDS scales and sub-scales.
26   See the appendix for the full list of MVPI scales and sub-scales.
27   See the appendix for the full list of TAIS factors. Learn more about the TAIS at: www.taisinventory.com.

and poor temperament—and it does so through an assessment of twenty attentional and interpersonal psychological factors.

"What makes TAIS so useful is the fact that the concentration skills and interpersonal abilities the inventory measures have an obvious and very direct link to virtually all performance situations," writes Dr. Nideffer in the article "Measuring the Building Blocks of Performance[28]." "It is this, combined with the fact preferred concentration and interpersonal styles become very trait like under pressure, that makes TAIS a valuable tool when working with individuals who must perform at very high levels and those who must perform under a lot of pressure."

2. Engage in a 360-Degree Feedback Assessment

While personality assessments are designed to measure traits, which are relatively stable indicators of the inherent leanings in our personality, 360-degree feedback focuses on assessing our behaviors.

Dr. Marshall Goldsmith—a widely renowned and award-winning executive coach, thought leader, and pioneer of the 360-degree feedback method—spearheaded a study examining how participating in a 360-feedback process impacted more than 11,000 managers[29]. Convincingly, his results showed that almost 75 percent of participants had experienced some form of improvement following this exercise.

Despite these impressive results, 360s can also cause harm to leaders and organizations alike if conducted incorrectly. Tales of nightmarish multi-rater feedback projects exist in many organiza-

---

28   Robert M. Nideffer, "TAIS Inventory » Measuring the Building Blocks of Performance," TAIS Inventory, accessed August 20, 2018, http://www.taisinventory.com/measuring-the-building-blocks-of-performance/.

29   Marshall Goldsmith and Howard Morgan, "Leadership Is a Contact Sport: The 'Follow-up Factor' in Management Development," *strategy+business, https://www.strategy-business.com/article/04307?gko=a260c.*

tions. To maximize the benefits of this approach, it is important to adhere to the following "best practices."

A. Many Consulting Firms Provide a 360-Degree Feedback Tool. Make Sure You Ask Critical Questions About How Their Specific Tool Was Developed

For example, ask the potential provider how the questions included in their instrument were created? Did they conduct any preliminary research to test for reliability/validity? On what populations did they test their tool? Regardless of your preference for how these questions are answered, it is important that they are asked so you can make an informed decision about the applicability and potential limits of the 360 tool.

B. Use 360-Degree Feedback for Development, Not for Performance Management

There can be numerous negative and unintended consequences to using 360s for determining bonuses or employment status. If employees believe their jobs are at risk for submitting negative feedback about their supervisors, they may hesitate to be honest in their appraisals. Instead, the best and most truthful feedback occurs when the individuals perceive the process as helping others grow and develop in their careers.

At the same time, if the 360 results affect performance pay or promotional opportunities for leaders, this can spark several negative reactions. First, leaders will likely and understandably be more resistant and defensive towards the feedback because of how it affects their salary and/or potential career trajectory. It may also provoke them to explicitly or implicitly pressure their employees to provide positive feedback. Remove these barriers by focusing 360-feedback on development.

C. Prepare the Candidate, Their Raters, and the Organization at Large

360s are most effective when everyone understands their purpose and how best to engage in the process. If you choose to undergo a 360, make sure that you clearly explain why you are pursuing this initiative and how your team and your colleagues will be involved. Make sure they understand the importance of providing honest and direct feedback and making it as specific as possible. Making these messages explicit maximizes the chances you will get the most out of this experience.

D. Make Sure the Process Includes a Self-Assessment

The best 360-degree feedback tools include a self-assessment, which provides an opportunity for the leader to compare his or her personal ratings to those provided by their colleagues. There are two important reasons for this comparison. First and foremost, it allows the leader to identify any potential blind spots. For example, if I rate myself a six out of seven on approachability, while my colleagues give me an average rating of two, then I have a significant a gap in my level of self-awareness, which creates an opportunity for exploration and growth. In other words, why do my colleagues see me as unapproachable whereas I feel the opposite?

A second and equally important benefit of including a self-assessment is that it affords the leader an opportunity to identify hidden strengths.

A client once shared with me that, even though she enjoyed public speaking, she thought she was terrible. Given its importance to her and to her success in her role, she asked if I would include some questions in an upcoming 360 to learn why she was so ineffective.

Surprisingly, it turned out that most people believed she possessed a real talent for public speaking. So why the discrepancy? As we talked through her results, we realized that when she would deliver a presentation, she selectively paid attention to negative as opposed to positive cues from the audience, such as looking for people distractedly using their cellphones when she was speaking. This immediately caused her to lose confidence. Thanks to the 360-feedback, she began to welcome new opportunities to speak instead of shying away from them, as she had done in the past.

In repositioning her perspective, she became much more visible, and in showing others the depth of her passion, insight, and ability to think quickly on her feet, she advanced significantly within the ranks. Eventually she accepted a forward-facing role that allowed her to regularly speak in front of groups, which was exactly what she wanted to do.

In comparing her perception of her public speaking ability to how others saw it, she was able to recognize that she was overly self-critical and it was actually a core strength of hers that was previously hidden.

Even though a lot of us who undergo a 360-degree assessment tend to focus on the negative feedback and where we can improve, discovering hidden strengths is an equally important benefit of the process; one that can help us uncover and capitalize on our unrealized potential.

E. Don't Take it Personally

When going through a 360-degree process, it's critical to approach it with an open mind. Instead of feeling down about any negative feedback received, see it for what it is: an opportunity to make sure our impact matches our intentions.

As we saw with my client, Susan, at the beginning of this chapter, these assessments provide an excellent means of exploring our actions through the eyes of the people around us. While Susan thought she was being supportive, her team members perceived her as being a micromanager.

Once we see and understand the gaps in our awareness, we can and should look to others for insight into how we can improve while still allowing ourselves the freedom to be who we are. This last point is important because the more authentic we make our solutions, the more likely we are to adhere to those strategies moving forward.

F. Follow-Up is Critical

The research conducted by Marshall Goldsmith and his colleagues also showed that the leaders who discussed their 360-feedback results with their direct reports and peers exhibited significantly better performance improvements than those who did not. This suggests that follow-up is very beneficial to a successful 360-degree process.

When following up with your colleagues, consider these three steps to ensure a positive and productive discussion:

1. Thank the respondents for investing their time and energy into providing you with their feedback.

2. Share your findings with respondents. If you are uncomfortable with complete transparency (which I highly recommend), at least share the key highlights and themes. This lets people know that their investment was not wasted and that you took the process seriously.

3. Inform everyone about your key takeaways and the positive changes you are looking to make moving forward. Better yet, enlist their support by asking them to let you know when you are slipping back into old habits. This final act requires considerable vulnerability and creates a powerful moment between a team and their leader. In publicly committing to making changes, you encourage those around you to support you and consequently maximize your chances of success.

G. Partner with a Coach

A study published in *Leadership & Organization Development*, which involved almost three hundred executives, concluded "that the combination of multi-rater feedback and individual coaching does increase leadership effectiveness up to 60 percent and beyond according to direct report and peer post-survey feedback[30]." In addition, the author noted a preliminary indication that the higher the number of coaching sessions, the greater the overall improvement.

When given the opportunity to discuss feedback results, ideally with someone trained in the administration of 360-degree feedback assessments, individuals are more likely to see sustained positive behavioral change. These conversations allow the participant to sift through and make sense of the large amount of data collected, while helping the leader focus on key strengths and opportunities for development.

---

30   E. C. Thach, "The impact of executive coaching and 360 feedback on leadership effectiveness," *Leadership & Organization Development Journal* 23, no. 4 (2002): 205-214, eftab720http://dx.doi.org/10.1108/01437730210429070.

3. Improve How We Deliver Feedback

When bestselling author Douglas Stone asks audiences around the world about their most difficult conversations, the most common answer is "giving or receiving feedback." Stone's twenty-two years of experience with the Harvard Negotiation Project, as well as his work as a lecturer at Harvard Law School, have given him considerable insight into the missteps people make in these discussions.

In his book *Thanks for the Feedback: The Science and Art of Receiving Feedback Well*, which he co-authored with colleague Sheila Heen, Stone explains that one of the reasons we all struggle with feedback is because we often fail to recognize that there is more than one type. In fact, when he and I spoke, he explained that there are three types of feedback, and each type is used for a different purpose[31]. "In order to better equip ourselves to navigate these conversations," says Stone, "it is important to understand these differences."

A. Appreciation

This feedback acknowledges others for their efforts and is often represented by statements such as, "Excellent work on that project." Or, "I appreciated all of the extra support you provided during that presentation."

B. Coaching

This is the dominant form of feedback used by executives and organizations, and can involve exploring opportunities for improvement. Examples include: "Based on what you learned while working with this client, what do we need to do when working with them in the

31   Craig Dowden, "How to Become Fluent in the Three Languages of Feedback," *Financial Post*, October 25, 2017, http://business.financialpost.com/executive/leadership/how-to-become-fluent-in-the-three-languages-of-feedback.

future?" or "What can we do better next time to avoid missing a deadline?"

C. Evaluation

This tells you where you stand in relation to your peer group or performance expectations. For example, "we set a target for 20 percent increased top-line sales in that channel this year. Unfortunately, we only hit 15 percent." Or, "You successfully completed the four continuous education courses you put on your development plan for this year."

As straightforward as this may sound, the challenge occurs when both parties are not clear on what form of feedback is needed—or what type of feedback is being offered.

For example, although we may feel we are offering coaching, our delivery style leads the other person to interpret it as an evaluation. This can create major frustration whereby the leader cannot understand why employees are not receptive to "coaching" while the team members feel that their boss is "always so judgmental."

Another form of mismatched conversation occurs when an employee reaches out to a manager for evaluation, yet receives appreciation instead. Consider the following exchange:

Employee: "I would like to be in the running for that promotion you talked about in our team meeting today. Where am I in relation to where I should be? What else could I be working on?"

Manager: "Don't worry about it. You're doing a great job. Just keep doing what you're doing."

Lastly, according to Stone, perhaps the most egregious mistake we make is when we combine coaching and evaluation in the same conversation.

"I could give you the best coaching advice in the history of the world," Stone told me, "but if I also include an evaluation in the same conversation, you are going to forget about the coaching because you are wondering, 'Why did I only get a rating of three out of five?'"

Given the last point, Stone notes that this (sometimes unintentional) combination of evaluation and coaching leads to tremendous amounts of lost learning opportunities. This is also why it is essential to use 360-feedback processes as a developmental, rather than evaluative, tool. Otherwise, all of the beneficial coaching and performance feedback will likely not be heard.

Another major issue raised by Stone is that executives rarely—if ever—use appreciation.

"Studies conducted by the (US) Department of Labor found that over 90 percent of workers felt under-appreciated," said Stone. "In addition, almost half of the people who left their jobs voluntarily say the reason they left is that they felt under-appreciated. To me, this shows that lack of appreciation is a serious issue."

By becoming fluent in the three languages of feedback, and developing and enhancing our skills in their delivery, we can learn how to turn difficult conversations into engaging ones.

IMPROVING PERFORMANCE REVIEWS

Performance reviews provide an excellent opportunity to receive feedback in terms of how we are doing relative to expectations. However, research shows that employees and managers strongly dislike these types of discussions, as each party often leaves the exchange feeling disappointed and frustrated. Informal feedback, on the other hand, reduces the stigma and makes it more a part of an everyday conversation. Don't fear the feedback!

When it comes to improving the feedback process, consider inviting your employees to take the reins and conduct their own do-it-yourself (DIY) performance review, preferably on a monthly basis.

This more frequent and employee-led approach is valuable on multiple levels, allowing feedback to

- become less threatening through familiarity,
- provide opportunity for real-time change and improvement, and
- become a part of your culture rather than an annual or semiannual event.

Perhaps the most important and distinct advantage is that it invites your employees to bring up their areas of challenge, which takes the burden off of you as the leader. In addition, it can even shed light on unexpected issues.

For instance, you may be preparing for a performance review with an employee, and have a list of points to cover. While a lot of it is positive, you feel some of the items may be challenging to deliver. Now, instead of delving into your list right away, turn to your employee and say, "I'd love to hear your thoughts. Where do you think things are going well? What do you think you might be able to do better?"

In answering, your team member may well address many of the items on your list, including some things you may not have previously considered. It is an excellent opportunity to identify hidden strengths while also raising your attention to areas of struggle that you may not have been aware of.

Also, it takes advantage of the reciprocity principle. By affording your employees the opportunity to take the lead on crafting their own performance review, it maximizes the chances that they will be open to hearing your comments and observations when the time comes.

This approach also provides a valuable opportunity for you to ascertain the levels of self-awareness within your team members. If an employee is lacking in self-awareness, you may want to monitor his or her performance more closely and coach around any blind spots you observe.

It should be noted that some of the largest organizations in the world are now looking to get rid of annual or semiannual performance reviews altogether and, instead, make feedback conversations an ongoing, embedded part of company culture.

Emerging research seems to support this shift, suggesting that annual performance reviews are outdated, stressful for employees, and time consuming for managers. In 2016, Adobe surveyed 1,500 office workers in the United States and found that 88 percent went through the standard performance review process, with written reviews, rankings, and ratings on a regular basis. Managers reported spending an average of seventeen hours per employee preparing for a performance review, with very little perceived return on investment[32]. In fact, 59 percent of the survey respondents reported these reviews had no impact on how they did their jobs. Instead, the process created stress, drove employees into needless competition with each other, and sometimes resulted in tears or employees quitting outright.

What workers are looking for, the study asserts, is "a collaborative process with regular and qualitative feedback."

In 2012, Adobe eliminated its annual performance review, instead opting for what it calls the "Check-In," a process that "focuses on two-way dialogue between manager and employee on an ongoing basis rather than heavy process and formal rankings."

Since implementing this model, Adobe estimates that it has saved more than 80,000 manager hours per year, which is the equivalent of forty full-time employees. With the growth in headcount since that time, the company estimates it saves over 100,000 manager hours per year and is now demonstrating higher retention, employee engagement, and stronger performance management.

---

32 Colleen Rodriguez, "Performance Review Peril: Adobe Study Shows Office Workers Waste Time and Tears," Adobe Newsroom, January 11, 2017, http://news.adobe.com/press-release/corporate/performance-review-peril-adobe-study-shows-office-workers-waste-time-and.

4. Know Why We Sometimes Act Out of Character and What to Do About It—The Adventures of Captain Kirk and Mr. Spock[33]

No matter how we plan to act in any given situation—being patient when someone is angry at us, for instance, or calm in the face of chaos—we can act out of character when the actual event takes place, despite our best intentions.

This occurs because of an interesting mental dichotomy that I often refer to as "Spock Brain" versus "Kirk Brain."

The Spock brain is our more rational self. It assesses situations from a cold, analytical standpoint and states, "This is how I *will* behave in X situation."

However, when we are *in* that situation, the Kirk Brain—our emotional self—emerges and overrides that analysis, often provoking us to react on emotion rather than logic.

Here's a quick example. Say you were to observe one team member openly berating another in the break room. How would you react in this situation?

When I ask audiences this question, the vast majority says something to the effect of, "I would step in and stand up for the person being yelled at." Yet, when I ask the audience how often this actually happens, very few, if any people can come up with an example.

Even though Spock predicts we are going to behave one way, Kirk shows up and ultimately derails our noble intentions.

It is also important to note that the process does not stop there. Because we have just acted out of character, we feel considerable

---

33 Readers are highly encouraged to check out the book *Blind Spots: Why We Fail to Do What's Right and What to Do About It* by Max Bazerman and Ann E. Tenbrunsel, which provides a comprehensive and thought-provoking investigation into this subject.

conflict. This necessitates a different interpretation. So, when we leave the situation, Spock reemerges to rationalize the choice that we made so we can continue to think of ourselves in an idealistic way.

Statements such as "There was no point in stepping in, it wouldn't have made a difference," or, "I'll just talk with them later, after they've calmed down" provide justification to ourselves.

Given this ethical blind spot, what can we do? Rather than trying to *think* through what we would do; instead, we need to focus on how we would *feel* in the situation and how those feelings may influence our course of action. Acknowledging our likely emotional reaction allows us to better orient ourselves when these situations occur, making us aware of the triggers and pressures we may feel so that we can manage them accordingly.

Another valuable exercise is to identify specific situations or people that may trigger our Kirk brain. Reflecting on past experiences where we acted out of character may be invaluable to discovering this information. Do we have problems with Lisa in Accounting? Are we caught off guard during our budgetary reviews? Being aware of contextual cues that can lead us astray empowers us to better prepare for these circumstances.

Key Decision Worksheet

Key decision: _____
(e.g.: Invest in new project management software)

Expected outcome: _____
(e.g.: 100 percent company visibility and alignment on all projects)

Why I am making this decision:

1. _____
   (e.g.: Project miscommunication is costing X in lost hours, clients are unhappy, work flow is disorganized, profitability is down X percent, etc.)

2. _____

3. _____

Factors to consider:

1. _____
   (e.g.: Will the cost of company-wide access to this platform be less than the current cost of project miscommunication?)

2. _____
   (e.g.: Will this platform take the place of multiple platforms currently in use?)

3. _____

Key assumptions along with corresponding rationale:

1. _____
   (e.g.: Project miscommunication is costing an estimated $1.2 million loss annually. The platform is $30,000 annually. The company states it will save at least half of our losses.)

2. _____
   (e.g.: Everyone will be trained on this platform, and all information moved to this platform, by six months after implementation.)

One year later [DATE]: _____

Did this decision result in the expected outcome? _____

Yes or No? Why or why not?

WATCH YOURSELF AND LEARN

One method for building self-awareness comes from Peter Drucker, one of the most highly respected management thinkers of the twentieth century.

"Whenever you make a key decision or take a key action," he states in his book *Managing Oneself*, "write down what you expect will happen. Nine or twelve months later, compare the actual results with your expectations."

In other words: watch yourself and learn.

In practical terms, this means that whenever you are faced with a major decision, write down all of the factors you are considering as well as the key factors that led you to a particular course of action. I have included a sample Key Decision Worksheet for your reference and use on the previous page.

Another great approach comes from the executive development program at Kenan-Flagler School of Business at the University of North Carolina. Two questions they ask their incoming executive MBA students are: "Tell me about one of your greatest successes and what role you played in its achievement?" Followed immediately by, "What would have happened if you did nothing?"

Sometimes we can obtain an amazing result through pure luck that might have happened without any involvement from us. Conversely, we may do all the right things and still not get the best outcomes. The point of the process is less about "what" happens and more about understanding "why" it happens—in codifying our motivations for a decision, we create a means by which we can go back and assess our process, learning just as much from our successes (what to do) as we do from our setbacks (what not to do).

5. Take Time for Self-Reflection

While the self-reflection exercise of "Watch Yourself and Learn" is helpful in building self-awareness, mapping out major decisions is also a relatively rare opportunity. Self-reflection should not be limited to significant events; it yields the most benefit when it is a daily routine. It provides leaders with the necessary time to contemplate and strategize to ensure that they are on track and achieving the things most important to them.

> The point of the process is less about "what" happens and more about understanding "why" it happens—in codifying our motivations for a decision, we create a means by which we can go back and assess our process, learning just as much from our successes (what to do) as we do from our setbacks (what not to do).

Since he is an early riser, one CEO told me he builds in time for self-reflection at the beginning of each day before anyone gets to the office[34], and he is very protective of that space in his calendar. Just as he would not haphazardly cancel crucial meetings with key clients or stakeholders, he understands that he is his most important strategic partner.

When I first introduce this exercise to clients, a common objection I receive is "I don't have time for this." This is not surpris-

---

34 Craig Dowden, "The Source president Charles Brown: 'I get to work at 6:30 a.m. to have time to reflect, so I don't just react.' Part 1," *Financial Post*, last modified May 10, 2017, https://business.financialpost.com/executive/leadership/the-source-president-charles-brown-i-get-to-work-at-630-a-m-to-have-time-to-reflect-so-i-dont-just-react.

ing. When our lives already seem full to overflowing, adding one more task may seem like the straw that will break us. Yet self-reflection, when done regularly, actually saves time because it allows us to consider what is truly important and where our real priorities lie.

Laura Vanderkam, a columnist for *The Wall Street Journal*, put it succinctly in her article on challenging and reframing our way of thinking:

"Instead of saying 'I don't have time' try saying 'it's not a priority,' and see how that feels. Often, that's a perfectly adequate explanation. I have time to iron my sheets, I just don't want to. But other things are harder. Try it: 'I'm not going to edit your résumé, sweetie, because it's not a priority.' 'I don't go to the doctor because my health is not a priority.' If these phrases don't sit well, that's the point. Changing our language reminds us that time is a choice. If we don't like how we're spending an hour, we can choose differently[35]."

It is important to realize that practicing self-reflection may be hard initially, as our first inclination may be to do something tactical, something that feels urgent. However, we need to come to terms with the fact that building in this time is the same as building in time for any other vital activity, like exercise or family. Its payoffs only increase through repetition and routine.

No one is going to make you take time for self-reflection. You simply need to schedule it and treat it like any other high priority business objective. Even if you only have fifteen minutes a day to dedicate to self-reflection, the more you honor that time, the more likely you are to continue that practice in the future.

If you are unsure what to ask yourself during your daily reflection time, here are some potential questions to get you started:

- What is my biggest priority right now?

---

35   Laura Vanderkam, "Are You As Busy As You Think?" *The Wall Street Journal*, February 22, 2012, https://www.wsj.com/articles/SB10001424052970203358704577237603853394654.

- What is my most important goal for today?

- How will I know I was successful today?

- Who is one person I need to speak with today?

- What is the area in which I need to improve most today?

6. Ask for Informal Feedback

For leaders, there is nothing preventing us from asking our colleagues, stakeholders, and customers how we are performing. A major bonus is that it is an easy and inexpensive way to see how we are doing.

Zenger Folkman discovered that "leaders who ask for feedback are perceived more positively than those who simply are good at giving feedback," adding that, "The ideal is to do both[36]." A leader who is willing to ask for specific feedback is both demonstrating how others should ask for feedback and how others should receive it, ultimately creating a culture where employees feel safe to follow suit.

In a subsequent study, these same researchers reported that leaders who asked for and acted on feedback were rated as significantly better in their roles[37]. In fact, a perfect linear trend emerged; the more leaders asked for and acted on feedback, the better their performance. Those leaders who were in the top ten percentile when it came to asking for and acting on feedback from others were rated in the ninetieth percentile of leadership effectiveness.

---

36 Jack Zenger, et al., "The Powerful Paradox: How to Make Feedback a Gift," Zenger|Folkman, 2015, http://zengerfolkman.com/wp-content/uploads/2015/04/Feedback-The-Powerful-Paradox.pdf.
37 "The Feedback Issue," Talent Quarterly, accessed December 5, 2018, http://www.talentstrategygroup.com/application/third_party/ckfinder/userfiles/files/TQ5 - The Feedback Issue.pdf.

Those Who Ask and Act on Feedback are Significantly Better Leaders

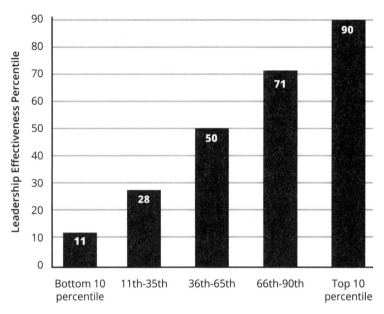

Asks for and Acts on Feedback from Others

"Feedback is a powerful tool that, if utilized with skill, can leverage the effectiveness of every leader," the firm concluded. "If you want to be highly skilled at providing others with feedback … then develop the habit of regularly asking others for feedback about yourself. It appears that in the process of getting feedback, we become much better at giving feedback and much more inclined to regularly do it."

Examples of Feedback Questions

When asking for feedback, it is important not to blindside your team members with questions. Give them time to reflect and provide a response. Most importantly, when asking these questions, explain why this feedback is critical to you (e.g. I want to be at my best) and how the person you are asking is important in terms of helping you in achieving your goals.

The following are some potential questions you can ask various audiences to receive feedback on how you are doing:

- What is one thing you would like me to

    □ continue doing?

    □ stop doing?

    □ start doing?

- If you were the leader of this team, what's the first thing you would do or change?

- Are you getting enough of my time? How much of my time do you need?

- How empowered do you feel?

- How comfortable are you in making decisions when I'm not around? What would make you feel more comfortable?

- How much autonomy do you have? How much do you want?

THE SELF-AWARENESS THOUGHT LEADER: MARSHALL GOLDSMITH

One of the best examples of how to be self-aware comes from top-rated executive coach Dr. Marshall Goldsmith and his story of the "But" Jar.

In our day-to-day conversations, there is one word that we say with regularity that does a tremendous job of uninspiring people: the use of the word "but."

"Joe, you did a great job on that presentation, but ..." Or

"That's a nice idea for the client, but …"

You might as well take a marker and scratch through the first part of the sentence, because anything said before "but" is essentially unheard. The use of "but" raises the listener's defensiveness because they sense that the real message only occurs after that word.

Goldsmith discusses the power of the word "but," and suggests that instead of using it, we replace it with the word "and."

"You did a great job on that presentation, Joe, and I'd like to see how it would look if we include the figures from the Smith account." Or,

"That's a nice idea for the client, and I wonder how they're going to receive it given the timeline?"

Instead of being dismissive, "and" validates the first part and builds a relationship with the listener instead of putting him or her on guard.

With this in mind, Goldsmith set himself on a mission to remove the word "but" from his vocabulary through the use of a "But" Jar.

Every time he used the word "but," he explained to his friends and colleagues, he wanted them to fine him, and that fine was kept in the "But" Jar.

This system served a couple of purposes. First, it raised his awareness of his use of the word, and secondly, it gave people in his life permission to confront him about it. And it was fun for them, too. They were motivated to look for the word and it created a sense of community and support.

I was so inspired by Goldsmith's story, in fact, that I took it on as a personal project for a full year, tasking my team to help me eliminate "but" from my vocabulary. Once I became aware of the power of the word, I was amazed at how often I used it. The exercise not only helped improve my communication skills, it also provided an excellent opportunity to build more self-awareness.

SELF-AWARENESS ON A CORPORATE SCALE: BLOCKBUSTER AND NETFLIX

Two years after opening their virtual doors and three years before they posted their first profits, Netflix CEO, Reed Hastings, and CFO, Barry McCarthy, flew to Dallas, Texas, to meet with Blockbuster CEO, John Antioco, to propose a partnership.

"Reed had the chutzpah to promote to them that we would run their [Blockbuster's] brand online and they would run [Netflix] brand in the stores and they just about laughed us out of their office," said McCarthy in a 2008 interview with The Unofficial Stanford Blog[38]. "At least initially, they thought we were a very small, niche market. Gradually over time, as we grew our market, his thinking evolved but initially they ignored us and that was much to our advantage."

Hastings made that proposal in 2000, when Blockbuster was pretty much at the top of its game. No other video rental organization came close to its number of locations, customers, and revenue, so when this little startup came in offering a partnership for a mere $50 million, it may not seem surprising that Antioco had to hold back a laugh.

Yet, the marketplace was changing, and while Netflix still had a lot of kinks to work out, the company was clearly looking toward the future. Meanwhile, Blockbuster was content to continue along with the status quo, adhering to the mantra, "If it ain't broke, why fix it?"

---

38   "Innovate Presents Barry McCarthy, Chief Financial Officer of Netflix," interview by the Unofficial Stanford Blog, audio, http://tusb.stanford.edu/2008/01/barry_mccarthy_chief_financial.html.

That changed in 2004 when Antioco and his team saw the writing on the wall and finally entered the online DVD rental market, launching Blockbuster's Total Access program. At the same time, he pushed the company to drop late fees, which was one of the key reasons Netflix was gaining ground. However, trying to push both of these major changes at once, at a combined cost of $400 million to the company, was where things went south. Members of the board pushed back on Antioco and he was ultimately fired, replaced by Jim Keyes who ditched both of Antioco's efforts and turned his attention back to the brick and mortar model.

"Clearly our spending on that one channel was exceeding our returns," said Keyes in regard to the Total Access program during a company earning's call[39].

"If I could turn back the clock, I might focus on the online business for a few more years and then drop late fees.[40] Both were the right thing to do, but doing them simultaneously increased costs and made a bitter pill for investors."

Despite later efforts to launch a program similar to Netflix, it was Blockbuster's lack of self-awareness that ultimately led to its eventual downfall. It was unable to see past its dominant position in the market to a time when its well-oiled business model might start to break down. Though still in its nascent stages, online video was becoming increasingly popular in 2000. In both jumping on that wave and simultaneously taking advantage of Blockbuster's Achilles'

---

39   Austin Carr, "Blockbuster Bankruptcy: A Decade of Decline," *Fast Company*, July 30, 2012, https://www.fastcompany.com/1690654/blockbuster-bankruptcy-decade-decline.

40   John Antioco, "How I Did It: Blockbuster's Former CEO on Sparring with an Activist Shareholder," *Harvard Business Review*, August 1, 2014, https://hbr.org/2011/04/how-i-did-it-blockbusters-former-ceo-on-sparring-with-an-activist-shareholder.

heel by eliminating late fees, Netflix swooped past the cumbersome giant and took the lead in the video race.

When Blockbuster finally went bankrupt in 2010, Netflix was valued at $28 billion—about ten times what Blockbuster was worth in its heyday. And it appears to have learned from Blockbuster's mistakes as well. Netflix continues to maintain a high degree of self-awareness by continually studying its customer data and adjusting its business model accordingly. For example, it has started creating its own content with TV shows and movies while also providing its more than 115 million subscribers worldwide with viewer ratings for each of the titles in its enormous catalogue[41].

41   —as of 2017.

PILLAR 2

CIVILITY

When once the forms of civility are violated, there remains little hope of return to kindness or decency.

—Samuel Johnson

After hearing me speak at a workshop about the importance of common courtesies, a senior executive later told me how a key piece of research I shared helped him solve a curious and potentially fatal issue that his department was facing.

His unit, he explained, was well-known for its incredibly high-quality work and commitment to consistently delivering results on time, yet its relationship with clients and stakeholders was terrible. Every interaction tended to be tense and abrasive, and no one could figure out why.

Following my presentation, he and his team decided to examine the emails sent by every member of the group, both to their clients as well as to each other, since it was their predominant form of communication. In doing so, they discovered a possible source of the issue: the exchanges did not include polite language very often. There was rarely a "Hello" or "Thank you for sending this along" or "I hope all is well." Instead, it was "Send this," "Need that," or "Update received."

Apparently, his employees felt that niceties "just got in the way" and were an "unnecessary waste of time." A recent internal workshop on email efficiency further reinforced this misguided idea. In their eyes, the work was what mattered most and it was more important to focus on delivering quality rather than "being nice."

With this revelation, the focus immediately turned to incorporating polite language into internal and external communications. Nothing over the top, just short phrases such as "Thanks so much," "Please," and "It was a pleasure." As a result, their relationships flourished and their overall performance increased to an even higher level. The executive was amazed at how something so small as saying "thank you" could deliver such powerful results.

> **MAKE THE WORLD A BETTER PLACE**
> A survey revealed that 95 percent of respondents felt that the world would be a better place if we said "please" and "thank you" more often. That is an extraordinary figure, and a bold statement on the profound need for more civility in all areas of life, not just the workplace.

DEFINING INCIVILITY

According to Drs. Christine Pearson and Christine Porath, two internationally recognized authorities on the topic, incivility is defined as "The exchange of seemingly inconsequential inconsiderate words and deeds that violate conventional norms of workplace conduct."

Considerable[42] research conducted by these and other experts with both supervisors and front line employees has identified the most common forms of incivility, including[43]:

- Neglecting to turn off cellphones

- Talking behind someone's back

- Paying little or no attention to an expressed opinion

- Taking credit for someone else's work or ideas

- Making demeaning remarks

- Blaming others rather than accepting responsibility

- Checking email or texting messages during a meeting

- Using email to send a difficult message to avoid facing the individual

- Not saying "please" or "thank you"

- Not listening during a meeting or conversation

- Talking over/down to someone

---

42   Christine M. Pearson, and Christine Porath, *The Cost of Bad Behavior: How Incivility Is Damaging Your Business and What to Do about It* (New York: Portfolio, 2009).

43   Thomas G. Reio, and Joanne Sanders-Reio, "Thinking About Workplace Engagement," *Advances in Developing Human Resources* 13, no. 4 (2011): 462-78, doi:10.1177/1523422311430784.

THE SCIENCE OF UNCIVIL LEADERSHIP

The Science of Uncivil Leadership:

1. Desire for Retribution

2. Impaired Performance

3. Lowered Team Spirit

4. Decreased Employee Engagement/Commitment

5. Poorer Physical Health

Although these examples of uncivil behaviors may not seem particularly egregious, their perceived insignificance makes them an even larger threat to organizational culture, as these actions may be normalized or understood as acceptable conduct. They may also be more easily dismissed as "not a big deal," which can prolong and intensify their negative effects[44]. Research shows the numerous and powerful consequences that happen when incivility is present in our organizations.

1. Desire for Retribution

An astounding 94 percent of people who feel they have been treated disrespectfully attempt to "get even" with the offender[45]. This includes actions such as "forgetting" to forward an email or passing along an urgent message. Additionally, 88 percent of people get even with the

---

44   While no one appreciates incivility, individuals who are high in conscientiousness are especially susceptible to its negative effects, suggesting that many high-potential employees (those with a heightened level of concern for doing their job well, thoroughly, and vigilantly) suffer from it even more strongly.

45   Christine M. Pearson, and Christine Porath, *The Cost of Bad Behavior: How Incivility Is Damaging Your Business and What to Do about It* (New York: Portfolio, 2009).

organization. This latter finding means that we are either unable or choose not to differentiate between the individual who is being disrespectful and the organization that employs him or her. Essentially, we feel that the organization is a willing accomplice, since it is not doing anything to curb the behavior.

2. Impaired Performance

Considerable research suggests that incivility affects individual, team, and organizational performance in various ways. Approximately two-thirds of employees report that their performance declined as a result of being treated uncivilly. Similarly, almost half (48 percent) of employees exposed to co-worker incivility lowered their work effort, and 38 percent intentionally decreased their work quality[46].

In particular, incivility can affect:

A. Time Spent On Work Tasks

Uncivil behavior disrupts the amount of time people spend on their work. For example, targets often avoid the offending individuals at the office. They also tend to talk with colleagues about these issues and, not surprisingly, spend time worrying about the incident.

Research conducted by badbossology.com discovered that most employees spend ten or more hours of work time per month either complaining, or listening to others complain, about their supervisors, with almost one-third of those respondents spending twenty hours or more per month on this activity. This lack of focus and lost time decreases workplace morale and, ultimately, productivity.

Another unsettling statistic is that Fortune 1000 executives spend an average of seven weeks each year resolving employee-related

---

46   Christine M. Pearson, and Christine Porath, "The Price of Incivility," *Harvard Business Review*, June 11, 2015, https://hbr.org/2013/01/the-price-of-incivility.

conflicts. Given the link between disrespectful behavior and conflict, identifying means of increasing civility in the workplace brings tremendous potential gains to our productivity as well as to employee morale.

B. Creativity

Drs. Porath and Amir Erez constructed a series of brilliant experiments to examine how incivility affects creativity[47]. In one case, participants were treated rudely by a "stranger" (a member of the research team) on their way to the study. In another trial, recruits observed a fellow "participant" (once again, a confederate) being berated for being late.

Creativity declined in both cases, with participants coming up with 39 percent fewer ideas after their uncivil encounter (when compared to participants who were not treated disrespectfully), and those who observed incivility within their group saw their creativity diminish by 50 percent.

Equally, if not more interesting, was the fact that participants who experienced or witnessed incivility came up with ideas that were rated significantly less creative by external evaluators than those forwarded by their counterparts. For instance, when asked to identify possible uses for a brick, the poorly treated participants said "build a house" or "build a wall," while the respectfully treated group suggested "using it as a goalpost for a street soccer game" or "painting it and giving it as a gift."

Given the heightened importance of creativity in today's fast-paced and ever-changing environment, the implications of this research are clear.

---

47 Christine Porath, and Amir Erez, "Does Rudeness Really Matter? The Effects of Rudeness on Task Performance and Helpfulness," *Academy of Management Journal* 50, no. 5 (2007): 1181-197, doi:10.5465/amj.2007.20159919.

C. Helpfulness

In the same experiment, Porath and Erez also looked into whether witnessing or experiencing incivility affected the participants' tendency to help one another. Specifically, they tested whether participants would help a "stranger" (a research team member) in need.

So as not to seem like part of the study, the designated "stranger" waited outside of the room in which the experiment was taking place. When a participant emerged, the "stranger" would walk by and "accidentally" drop something.

Again, participants who were either a direct target of, or who had witnessed incivility were significantly less likely to offer assistance. As there was no relationship between the person in need and the people who demonstrated incivility earlier, this finding demonstrates how rudeness begets rudeness, and can set up a vicious cycle of paying negative behavior forward. One final point is also important to mention. When it comes to the impacts of uncivil behavior, the effects are virtually the same, regardless of whether the individual is the target or witness of the behavior. This has tremendous implications, as it suggests that uncivil behavior extends far beyond the situation in which it occurs.

3. Lowered Team Spirit

When compared to teams that rank in the bottom 10 percent on civility, those in the top 10 percent

- possess 26 percent more energy,

- are 30 percent more likely to feel motivated and enthusiastic about acquiring new skills and being exposed to new ideas,

- experience a 30 percent increase in feelings of vitality,

- express 36 percent more satisfaction with their jobs and are 44 percent more committed to their organizations, and

- receive significantly higher performance ratings (e.g. 20 percent improvement) from their superiors when compared to individuals who are part of the least civil teams in the organization[48].

4. Decreased Employee Engagement/Commitment

Research shows the tremendous costs of disrespectful behaviors on the desire of employees to remain with their organization[49]. In one study, 78 percent of participants indicated that their commitment to the organization declined following uncivil treatment[50]. Other research also suggests that targets of incivility tend to report lower levels of job satisfaction and a higher intent to quit their job[51] [52]. In fact, 12 percent leave as a result[53].

Disrespectful behaviors wreak havoc on engagement as well. Previous work revealed that high levels of face-to-face incivility

---

48 Christine M. Pearson, and Christine Porath, *The Cost of Bad Behavior: How Incivility Is Damaging Your Business and What to Do about It* (New York: Portfolio, 2009).

49 Thomas G. Reio, and Joanne Sanders-Reio, "Thinking About Workplace Engagement," *Advances in Developing Human Resources* 13, no. 4 (2011): 462-78, doi:10.1177/1523422311430784.

50 Christine M. Pearson, and Christine Porath, "The Price of Incivility," *Harvard Business Review*, June 11, 2015, https://hbr.org/2013/01/the-price-of-incivility.

51 Lisa M. Penney, and Paul E. Spector, "Job Stress, Incivility, and Counterproductive Work Behavior (CWB): The Moderating Role of Negative Affectivity," *Journal of Organizational Behavior* 26, no. 7 (2005): 777-96, doi:10.1002/job.336.

52 Sandy Lim et al., "Personal and Workgroup Incivility: Impact on Work and Health Outcomes," *Journal of Applied Psychology* 93, no. 1 (2008): 95-107, doi:10.1037/0021-9010.93.1.95.

53 Christine M. Pearson, and Christine Porath, "The Price of Incivility," *Harvard Business Review*, June 11, 2015, https://hbr.org/2013/01/the-price-of-incivility.

resulted in considerable reductions in employee engagement[54]. A recent intervention focused on enhancing civility found that reduced incidences of incivility were linked with increased engagement[55].

Incivility also reduces organizational citizenship behaviors (OCB), which are highly valued extra-role behaviors that extend above and beyond the call of duty (e.g., coming into work early or staying late to work on a project; assisting a colleague who needs help without any expectation in return)[56]. When workplace incivility leads to a decline in the emotional commitment employees feel toward their employer, research shows that OCBs decline along with it[57].

5. Poorer Physical Health

Negative relationships can also lead to damaging effects on our physical health. One provocative British study examined the impact of a negative versus positive supervisory style on the blood pressure readings of employees[58]. On alternate days, employees worked either with a manager with whom they had a positive relationship, or one with whom they had a negative relationship. Results revealed that blood pressure significantly spiked when employees worked with the "bad boss."

54 Thomas G. Reio, and Joanne Sanders-Reio, "Thinking About Workplace Engagement," *Advances in Developing Human Resources* 13, no. 4 (2011): 462-78, doi:10.1177/1523422311430784.
55 Katerine Osatuke et al., "Civility, Respect, Engagement in the Workforce (CREW)," *The Journal of Applied Behavioral Science* 45, no. 3 (2009): 384-410, doi:10.1177/0021886309335067.
56 Ibid.
57 Shannon G. Taylor et al., "Linking Workplace Incivility to Citizenship Performance: The Combined Effects of Affective Commitment and Conscientiousness," *Journal of Organizational Behavior* 33, no. 7 (2011): 878-93, doi:10.1002/job.773.
58 N. Wager et al., "The Effect on Ambulatory Blood Pressure of Working under Favourably and Unfavourably Perceived Supervisors," *Occupational and Environmental Medicine* 60, no. 7 (2003): 468-74, doi:10.1136/oem.60.7.468.

The implications of this innovative work were extended in another study that explored the longer-term health effects of working with a toxic leader. Conducted over a fifteen-year period, researchers were interested to determine the link, if any, between a bad boss and the risk of coronary problems[59]. Even after controlling for major risk factors such as perceived workload, activity level, education, social class, income, and supervisory status, the research indicated that employees who had a difficult relationship with their boss were significantly more likely to develop coronary heart disease or suffer a heart attack.

PRACTICING CIVIL LEADERSHIP

Practicing of Civil Leadership

1. Say "Please" and "Thank You"

2. Create a Team Charter

3. Model Positive Behavior

4. Watch Your Language

5. Put Away Electronic Devices

6. Encourage Feelings of Psychological Safety

7. Take Immediate Corrective Action When Warranted

---

59   Reiner Rugulies, and Ida Madsen, "Faculty of 1000 Evaluation for Managerial Leadership and Ischaemic Heart Disease among Employees: The Swedish WOLF Study," *F1000 - Post-publication Peer Review of the Biomedical Literature*, 2009. doi:10.3410/f.1153902.613958.

As the preceding review shows, even short-term exposure to disrespectful behavior has profound and troubling impacts. What can leaders do to foster a respectful workplace?

1. Say "Please" and "Thank You"

As we learned from the unintentionally brusque department at the beginning of this chapter, even when you're delivering the highest quality of work, the value of basic social niceties cannot be understated.

"People seem surprised to see how saying little things can be so powerful," said Harvard Business School professor Francesca Gino in an interview with *Harvard Business Review*[60]. Remarking on the results of a poll that suggested the workplace is the least thankful area of our lives (with only 15 percent of people saying "thank you" at work, compared to half saying it at home), Gino cited research she conducted with Adam Grant, in which they studied the impact of a simple expression of "thank you."

In their first experiment, participants were asked to review a cover letter submitted by a university student named "Eric" and email him their comments and suggestions. Shortly thereafter, Eric reached out to each of the participants with another request for help, except this time the participants received one of two very different emails.

In the first condition, Eric thanked the participants for reviewing his cover letter before asking for his next favor. In the second case, Eric just asked for feedback on another cover letter, without bothering to thank the person for their initial assistance.

---

60 Francesca Gino and Adam Grant, "The Big Benefits of a Little Thanks," *Harvard Business Review*, March 30, 2015, https://hbr.org/2013/11/the-big-benefits-of-a-little-thanks.

"What was striking to us," said Gino, "is that the percentage of people who helped more than doubled [66 percent] in the condition in which the person who participated in the study received the expression of gratitude from the student."

What was especially interesting about this research was the impact Eric's behavior also had on future requests for help from others.

In a second study, Grant and Gino provided the exact same scenario as in the first. In this case, however, the day after Eric's follow-up email, the participant received a new request for help from a different student who was looking for feedback on their cover letter. Once again, Eric's actions (e.g. whether or not he thanked the participant for their help) significantly impacted the willingness of the participants to help another person. For those whom Eric thanked, 55 percent agreed to help out the new student while only one-quarter of those in the "thankless" group were willing to volunteer assistance.

When we think about building a civil workplace, we often jump right to the costs of culture change: human resources, time, creating focus groups, and following up on the results. We also may wonder if we run the risk that, despite our best efforts, we might not get the buy-in we need from everyone involved. Civility does not need to start with a massive investment. It can start with something as simple as saying "thank you."

2. Create a Team Charter

Even when people are highly motivated to treat each other with respect, considerable variation may exist in terms of their level of understanding about what this means in practice. For example, in a survey aimed at determining how people interpret probabilistic words such as "often" and "possibly," researchers discovered that people not only broadly interpret general terms such as "real possibility" (with respondents giving a range of 20-80 percent likelihood that something with a "real possibility" will occur), they also do not agree that "always" means "100 percent of the time[61]." With such wide interpretations of seemingly obvious words like "always," are we surprised that there can be considerable variation in more ambiguous words like "civility?"

To curb any conflicts that may stem from misalignments of meaning, leaders can work with their team and within their organization to create common understandings of what "civility" means in day-to-day practice. This Team Charter can then be referenced in the event that actions or expectations are brought into question.

Two clients of mine, whom I'll call Chris and Jenna, were certainly in need of a basic Team Charter when we first met. In their case, the conflict arose from a misunderstanding around the phrase "team player."

When it came to the consulting practice they had started together, Chris and Jenna were each responsible for a different area, although they routinely needed to collaborate on creating joint solutions for clients. In this instance they had met with a client and pitched a solution that was so well received, a written proposal was requested for four o'clock the following Tuesday.

It was at this point that the seeds of conflict were sown. Chris was notoriously late in submitting materials—so much so that it had already created a significant strain on their relationship. With the deadline looming, Jenna worried that Chris wouldn't submit his work on time. And she was right. As the clock ticked closer to the

---

61 Andrew Mauboussin, and Michael J. Mauboussin, "If You Say Something Is 'Likely,' How Likely Do People Think It Is?" *Harvard Business Review*, July 3, 2018, https://hbr.org/2018/07/if-you-say-something-is-likely-how-likely-do-people-think-it-is.

deadline, no emails were forthcoming from Chris. By Tuesday at noon, with only four hours left to turn in their proposal, she gave up and wrote the entire proposal herself, stamped "draft" on it, and sent it to the client, cc'ing Chris on the email.

Ten minutes later, she received an angry phone call from Chris saying how she had "thrown him under the bus" and that she "wasn't a team player."

Now, Jenna understood that she risked not getting Chris' side of the proposal exactly right, but with the deadline only hours away, she thought she was being the ultimate team player by taking care of the proposal and getting it in on time. In fact, she felt she was doing the lion's share of the work and saving face for him by doing this. She had also purposefully written the word "draft" on the document and explicitly told the client that they welcomed feedback.

To Chris, this was not remotely close to his definition. To him, team players provide a united front; they work together so there are no surprises. Never would he forward a document to a client without seeking Jenna's feedback or input first.

In this scenario, as odd as it may seem, both Chris and Jenna are right. The other person is not being a team player. Here's the catch. The reason is that each of them is using a different operational definition. Faced with this realization, both Chris and Jenna worked together to create a mutually agreed definition, including behavioral expectations for the future. Their working relationship improved significantly and both felt respected and valued by the other.

An open discussion around the definition of common terms raises awareness and sensitivity toward the behaviors associated with them. In fact, teams that create Team Charters are 125 times more likely to address unacceptable team behaviors promptly, and thirty-nine times more likely to live by the norms and behaviors they have established. Consequently, teams with established Charters are forty-seven times more likely to work hard to build and maintain trust, and twenty-six times more likely to feel comfortable asking for help from each other when they are struggling or uncertain[62].

Another major advantage of this practice is that it empowers employees to hold each other accountable, which is highly desirable for team leaders. For example, if a group agrees that cellphone usage is not acceptable during face-to-face meetings, the next time a team member pulls one out during that restricted time, the other team members feel more comfortable reminding him or her about their mutual agreement. Furthermore, rather than being a punitive act, it is seen as protecting the core values of the group.

3. Model Positive Behavior

Russian novelist Leo Tolstoy famously stated, "Everyone thinks of changing the world, but no one thinks of changing himself[63]." Evidence suggests that following Tolstoy's proclamation can bring tremendous benefits to leaders and organizations. Based on their experience and research, McKinsey & Company estimate that half of all organizational transformation efforts fall short either because senior leaders fail to act as role models for change, or because people in the organization are allowed to defend the status quo[64].

In investigating the power of positive role models, female participants in a study were asked to deliver a speech to an audience. In one condition, the portrait of a well-known, high-ranking female

---

62 Linda J. Adams, "The Loyalist Team Assessments - Methodology, Findings, Data Reliability and Validation," August 2017, http://www.trispectivegroup.com/wp-content/uploads/2017/09/ASSESSMENT-RESEARCH-1.pdf.

63 Mark A. Bryan et al., *The Artist's Way at Work: Riding the Dragon* (New York: William Morrow, 1999), 160.

64 S. Keller, and C.Price, "Organizational health: The ultimate competitive advantage," *McKinsey Quarterly,* June 2011.

leader hung on the back wall. In the control condition, no portrait was used. When their speeches were assessed, it turned out that those who were exposed to the gender-specific role model spoke for significantly longer. More importantly, audience members rated these speeches as more impactful in terms of body language and fluency compared to their control group counterparts. These results demonstrate how the act of simply viewing a relatable role model can inspire the exhibition of stronger leadership behaviors[65].

The idea that the disrespectful behavior of senior leaders can and does encourage the expression of similar behaviors in their direct reports was supported by the findings of another study, which showed that one-quarter of managers admitted to acting disrespectfully towards others because their own supervisors treated them in a similar manner[66]. Given this relationship, the power of being a positive role model cannot be underestimated.

4. Watch Your Language

As often as we may have heard the phrase "watch your language" as kids, evidence suggests that its applicability extends into adulthood. Considerable research highlights how the words we use to describe situations and people can have profound impacts on our experience as well as on our levels of civility.

In one simple, yet powerful, experiment, John Bargh and his colleagues divided participants into two groups to complete the task of creating a sentence out of a set of jumbled words (for instance,

65   Ioana M. Latu et al., "Successful Female Leaders Empower Womens Behavior in Leadership Tasks," *Journal of Experimental Social Psychology* 49, no. 3 (2013): 444-48, doi:10.1016/j.jesp.2013.01.003.
66   Christine M. Pearson, and Christine Porath, "The Price of Incivility," *Harvard Business Review*, June 11, 2015, https://hbr.org/2013/01/the-price-of-incivility.

"rule," "respect," "golden," "the" becomes "respect the golden rule") [67]. One group was tasked with scrambled sentences with words relating to incivility, such as "intrude," "bother," "rude," and "infringe," while the other group was given scrambles with words of kindness/politeness, such as "patiently," "appreciate," and "courteous."

When they were finished solving the word scrambles, participants were asked to walk down the hall to receive their next set of instructions. When they arrived, they found that they had to wait while another "participant" (one of the researchers) engaged in a lengthy conversation with the lead experimenter. The researchers were interested to see how quickly the participants would wait before interrupting.

The results revealed that individuals who were primed with "rude" words interrupted significantly faster than those who received words associated with politeness. In fact, while the "rude" group tended to interrupt after about five minutes, the vast majority of the "polite" group did not interrupt at all and waited the full ten minutes of the staged conversation.

5. Put Away Electronic Devices

Leaders benefit from putting away their technology when meeting with others because it elevates the level of civility within their immediate sphere of influence. Better yet, leaders can enforce "smartphone-free" meetings and encourage others to follow suit.

One fascinating study documented the powerful debilitating impacts that these devices have on conversational and relational

---

67   John A. Bargh et al., "Automaticity of Social Behavior: Direct Effects of Trait Construct and Stereotype Activation on Action," *Journal of Personality and Social Psychology* 71, no. 2 (1996): 230-44, doi:10.1037//0022-3514.71.2.230.

dynamics[68]. In the first group, participants engaged in a fifteen-minute conversation with a stranger at an empty table. In a second group, a smartphone was placed in plain view. It is important to note that no one used the phone. It was just there.

Results showed that the mere presence of the phone significantly diminished the quality of connection between the two people as well as the level of trust. What's more, the impacts of the device were even more pronounced when people were engaged in meaningful/deeper conversations as opposed to casual ones.

This study raises a disturbing question about how our "technology manners" affect our relationships. How often do we put our phone on the table when meeting an employee? A potential customer? A friend? Unless absolutely necessary, this research cautions that the quality of connection and trust is likely significantly compromised.

In my coaching work, I regularly share this research. When executives are courageous and determined enough to practice this, they report incredible results. In particular, not only are they surprised about how differently they show up in their conversations with others, an even bigger revelation is how their conversational partners engage on a different level. This leads to deeper relationships and stronger trust bonds, which benefit all parties involved.

68   Andrew K. Przybylski, and Netta Weinstein, "Can You Connect with Me Now? How the Presence of Mobile Communication Technology Influences Face-to-face Conversation Quality," *Journal of Social and Personal Relationships* 30, no. 3 (2012): 237-46.

ELECTRONIC INCIVILITY

The negative effects of incivility extend far beyond interpersonal interactions[69]. Uncivil conduct is especially pronounced and rampant in online forums. Labeled the "online disinhibition effect," this refers to the phenomenon that people tend to say and do things online that they would not do in person[70].

Research has shown that disrespectful behaviors that occur through electronic communications exact the same toll as those delivered in person. In one study, participants were asked to complete a series of problem-solving tasks where the instructions and feedback were transmitted solely via email[71]. At different times, the supervisor would communicate in either a supportive manner (e.g. "I really appreciate your efforts on these tasks.") or in an uncivil manner (e.g. "Try these next tasks, genius.").

Unsupportive supervisory comments prompted significantly lower levels of energy and higher levels of negative affect when compared to supportive supervisory comments. More importantly, disrespectful interactions also contributed to significant declines in both performance and engagement.

69   Ibid.
70   Melanie Nguyen and Andrew J. Campbell, "Online Disinhibition Effect: Identity, Temporality, and Visual Cues," *PsycEXTRA Dataset*, no. 7 (2008): 321-26, doi:10.1037/e504592008-001.
71   Gary W.Giumetti et al., "What a Rude E-mail! Examining the Differential Effects of Incivility versus Support on Mood, Energy, Engagement, and Performance in an Online Context," *Journal of Occupational Health Psychology* 18, no. 3 (2013): 297-309, doi:10.1037/a0032851.

6. Encourage Feelings of Psychological Safety

Psychological safety is the degree to which employees feel comfortable taking an interpersonal risk at work[72]. When employees feel safe, they provide open and honest feedback without fear of reprisal. They are also more willing to speak up when mistakes occur. In fact, psychological safety leads to significant gains in learning, on-the-job performance, employee engagement, and creativity[73, 74, 75].

One way in which leaders can promote psychological safety within their teams and organizations is by suspending judgment and approaching situations and people with a learning mind-set. Rather than looking for problems or assigning blame, leaders should seek to understand others' perspectives.

Bestselling author Dr. Marilee Adams has spent her illustrious career teaching others how to ask more powerful questions and be more aware of their mind-sets. When we are in learning mode, we are open-minded, flexible, and connected. Judging, on the other hand, is associated with being closed, critical, and inflexible. When I spoke with her about whether one mind-set was preferred over the other, she emphasized that both are normal, noting that "judgmental" does not mean "judgment."

"We all need to make judgments," she said, adding that the judgmental mind-set is all about emotions, fear, survival, and protection.

---

72 Amy Edmondson, "Psychological Safety and Learning Behavior in Work Teams," *Administrative Science Quarterly* 44, no. 2 (1999): 350, doi:10.2307/2666999.
73 Ibid.
74 Amy C. Edmondson et al., "Disrupted Routines: Team Learning and New Technology Implementation in Hospitals," *Administrative Science Quarterly* 46, no. 4 (2001): 685, doi:10.2307/3094828.
75 Douglas R. May et al., "The Psychological Conditions of Meaningfulness, Safety and Availability and the Engagement of the Human Spirit at Work," *Journal of Occupational and Organizational Psychology* 77, no. 1 (2004): 11-37, doi:10.1348/096317904322915892.

"Although we need the judgmental part of our brain, we don't want to be ruled by it. Unfortunately, a large number of us do not realize that a lot of our thinking, acting, and feeling start with this judging mind-set."

To make the shift from judging to learning, Dr. Adams explains that we first need to recognize the mind-set in which we are operating in any given moment. If we are in judging mode, then we can train ourselves to ask "switching" questions such as, "How else could I think about this situation/person?"

Becoming aware of our mind-set and "switching" when necessary is the first and best move leaders can make to create a psychologically safe environment.

DR. ADAMS LEARNING AND JUDGING QUESTIONS

JUDGER	LEARNER
Blame	Responsibility
Either/Or Thinking	Both/And Thinking
Defends Assumptions	Questions Assumptions
Possibilities Limited	Possibilities Endless
Primary Mood: Protective	Primary Mood: Curious
Fears Differences	Values Differences
Feedback Perceived as Rejection	Feedback Perceived as Worthwhile
Listens for Right/Wrong	Listens for Facts
JUDGER QUESTIONS	**LEARNER QUESTIONS**
What's wrong?	What works?
Whose fault is it?	What am I responsible for?
What's wrong with me?	What do I want?
How can I prove I'm right?	What can I learn?
How will this be a problem?	What are the facts? What's useful about this?

Why is that person so stupid and frustrating?	What is the other person thinking, feeling, and wanting?
How can I be in control?	What's the big picture?
Why bother?	What's possible?

HANDLING REPORTS OF INCIVILITY

Leaders should recognize that there is tremendous pressure on individuals to not report incidents of incivility, not the least of which is the fear of retaliation or potentially suffering serious career setbacks. Additional research suggests that when employees report negative behaviors to their supervisors, only 18 percent of leaders take positive steps to address it. More commonly, the supervisor does nothing (40 percent) or their actions make the situation worse (42 percent)[76]. For instance, if we were to react to a report of incivility by acting embarrassed or even defensive, the team member who shared it may feel uncomfortable in bringing that kind of information to our attention again.

Successfully navigating these complex and powerful moments is a major challenge for even the most trained and experienced professional. Therefore, in cases where someone demonstrates the courage to openly express personal feelings and observations, it is crucial that the exchange take place in an emotionally supportive environment. For example, leaders can ask

---

76   Gary Nami and Ruth Namie, *The Bully at Work: What You Can Do to Stop the Hurt and Reclaim Your Dignity on the Job* (Naperville: Sourcebooks, 2009).

"What would you like (for me) to do in this situation?" and then open it up to collective problem solving.

Ultimately, when addressing uncivil behavior, leaders should follow up with both parties involved in the incident to outline the expectations moving forward. The consequences to the offender for failing to live up to these standards should also be clearly articulated. This ensures that the person at fault not only understands the unacceptability of the reported actions and what he or she is accountable for, it also shows the desired roadmap for future behavior. Employees also see there is accountability attached, which increases the likelihood that these incidents will be reported to the organization and its leadership in the future.

7. Take Immediate Corrective Action When Warranted

Disrespectful behaviors can emerge quickly and without warning, creating a critical decision point that leaders need to respond to in the moment. In many cases, they can miss this opportunity and "move on," hoping that ignoring the incident will make it go away and that it will eventually be forgotten.

Without an immediate response, however, the credibility of the leader and the broader organization will likely be seriously questioned, as inaction sends the (perhaps unintended) message that this behavior is tolerable and even acceptable. Additionally, the longer we wait to respond, the less precise both parties' recollections of the incident will be[77].

---

77   James A. Kulik, and Chen-Lin C. Kulik, "Timing of Feedback and Verbal Learning," *Review of Educational Research* 58, no. 1 (1988): 79, doi:10.2307/1170349.

If treating people with respect is truly a core value within our organizations, then incivility should be met with an immediate and decisive response. Failing that, people may understandably wonder whether these values are as important as advertised.

THE CIVIL CEO: DOUG CONANT

No one taught Doug Conant, former CEO of Campbell Soup Company, that handwriting thank you notes was an excellent way to boost employee morale and engagement. No one explained to him that people don't know what you're thinking—that you create better connections with others when you declare who you are and what you're about when you first meet. He was not, in fact, a star player at all when he began as a marketing assistant at General Mills in 1978. On his six-month review, his boss described his performance as "mediocre" and his boss's boss simply suggested that he find another job.

Yet Conant persisted, moving into another division where his general manager recognized him for his efforts, which gave him the confidence to grow into his role. As Conant worked his way up to the C-suite, he never forgot the hard lessons he learned early on, and was determined that he would approach his leadership with less severity and more civility.

"If people know that you're listening and that you want to work *with* them to achieve the desired outcome, they're far more responsive," Conant explained to me. "And if you want people to perform to high standards, you have to be clear about those standards while also being tender-hearted with people."

For Conant, this meant abiding by three Rules of Appreciation: be direct, celebrate often, and don't forget to write.

When it comes to the first rule, Conant says, "If there's one thing I encourage leaders to do right now, it's declare yourself to the people that report directly to you, one by one. The key is to be direct and take the mystery out of the relationship. When you do that, you can focus on doing the work and not managing the room."

The second rule, celebrate often, does not mean breaking out balloons and party hats for every success. Instead, it means appreciating others in simple, heartfelt ways for accomplishments that mean a lot to them, even if it's not a big deal to the rest of the company. Every day, Conant and his team looked for opportunities to celebrate employees, whether it was providing a pat on the back for reaching a goal or sending a handwritten congratulatory note for a promotion; which led to Conant's third rule—write and write often.

Despite all of his impressive achievements, Conant is perhaps best-known for the number of notes he has handwritten. Over the course of thirty years, Conant estimates he sent roughly 30,000 cards to employees, to everyone from maintenance to senior leadership. "Personal attention is underrated," says Conant. "Whether it's sharing a handwritten note or stopping by somebody's desk to acknowledge a job well done, however you can make it personal, you win."

CIVILITY ON A CORPORATE SCALE: PUBLIX SUPERMARKETS

"Make every customer's day a little better because they met you." Every Publix associate, whether a part-time front service clerk (cashiers and baggers) or full-time regional manager, memorizes and lives by this slogan. It is part of the supermarket's culture—one which has been celebrated on national and international levels for its loyalty, phenomenally low turnover rate (5 percent compared to the retail industry average of 65 percent), and the consistently happy customers that result from it.

At Publix, associates go out of their way to be helpful and, should a customer become dissatisfied, employees are trained to do what they can to "create a happily ever after." If this means re-frosting a cake, finding a specific brand of toothpaste, carrying bags to a car, or tracking down the right loaf of bread, Publix believes in treating customers with respect and civility.

Founded in 1930, in Winter Haven, Florida, Publix is the largest employee-owned company in the world, with more than 175,000 associates and 1,110 stores throughout the southeastern United States[78]. Publix attributes its success to both its admirable associate tenure (store managers are in their roles an average of twenty-five years) and very high customer satisfaction.

In 2016, *Fortune* magazine journalist Christopher Tkaczyk spent five days working in various departments across the organization to learn the secret behind why Publix "may have the happiest, most motivated workforce in America," as it has been consistently ranked in the top tier of supermarkets in the American Customer Satisfaction Index for more than twenty years.

It was the reporter's third day on the job and he was stationed in the bakery, where he had spent the pre-dawn hours helping his team make dozens of fresh loaves. Along with learning the ins and outs of bread making, cake decorating, and donut frosting, he was also getting "a crash course in world-class service"; training which was put to the test when an irate customer approached him about a sub-standard loaf of bread.

---

78 Christopher Tkaczyk, "Bag Boy Confidential: My Five Days of Working at Publix," *Fortune*, March 3, 2016, http://fortune.com/publix-best-companies/.

"You never have any bread with a thick crust like they do back in New York," the woman said to Tkaczyk, pressing her thumb into a soft loaf of wheat.

Instead of becoming defensive, Tkaczyk drew on his Publix training by immediately and respectfully engaging her in a discussion about something they had in common (e.g., New York), as he searched for a loaf with an acceptably hard crust. By the time he found it and handed it to her, she had visibly calmed down and even thanked him for the extra effort he had shown. As she left the bakery, he naturally thanked her for dropping by, adding, "Come back and see us again soon!"

This intense focus on respecting the customer, treating them with civility and with gratitude, is one of the core elements behind what makes Publix, one of the few private companies on the Fortune 500, so successful. In fact, this philosophy is encompassed in one of their six founding principles: "Respect the dignity of the individual[79]."

---

[79] "Lessons From Our Founder," Publix Super Markets, accessed August 20, 2018, http://corporate.publix.com/about-publix/culture/lessons-from-our-founder.

PILLAR 3

HUMILITY

Humility is not thinking less of yourself, but thinking of yourself less.

—Rick Warren, *The Purpose Driven Life*

Although Jack's career was defined by growing businesses, his management style was highly rigid. He was a micromanager most of the time and was known to routinely fly off the handle if his directives were not followed to the letter. The fact that his current employer was being positioned for an acquisition only exacerbated his natural tendencies for control. As a result, a 360-degree feedback of Jack's employees returned very low engagement scores, which were troubling both to the president as well as to potential investors.

The understanding that several key individuals who worked under Jack had recently left the organization raised additional red flags. Something had to be done and the company's president asked me if I could work with Jack.

Fortunately, Jack recognized this as an opportunity to make positive changes.

When we first discussed his approach, I asked him: "How do you think your team members experience you as a leader?"

He said it was a great question, and one he had not considered before. He was so focused on driving results that he had never really taken the human element into account.

As we further unpacked the question, Jack acknowledged that he could get angry and lash out with minimal provocation. He also admitted that he could become quite judgmental and berate people publicly. Up until this point, this approach had been a non-issue for him; it was simply necessary to get results and those who had a problem with him just needed to "suck it up."

Looking back on his behavior, he realized how this style created the low engagement scores and turnover issues he was facing.

Now the bigger question was, what was he was going to do about it? This led us to the heart of the matter.

"Have you ever apologized for these behaviors?" I asked him.

"Apologized?" he asked, perplexed by the question. "I don't think I've ever apologized for anything in my life."

Before this moment, an apology was a sign of weakness to Jack. And although his current situation made him open to the idea that apologizing could be a viable strategy, he struggled with what he could say. So, over the next couple of hours, we put together a script for how he could best express his thoughts.

The very next time he met with his team, he explained, "I recognize that I've been a really harsh driver for results, and the way I channel that is not good for any of you or for me. I'm sorry. That's not the type of leader that I want to be, and I can see now what I was doing. I'm working with a coach and I am hoping you can help me. From this day forward, you're going to see a change. However, if I fall back to 'Jack 1.0,' I want you to call me out. I need you to help me become a better leader and a better person."

The best part of my job is hearing and seeing how my work impacts others. After that meeting, I had the opportunity to speak one-on-one with members of Jack's team. They all mentioned how impressed they were with the courage he exhibited in standing in front of everyone and taking responsibility. Now, even when Jack makes a misstep, they sense that his heart is in the right place, and they feel more comfortable talking about their own challenges with him and with each other.

Of the feedback I received, one of the most powerful statements came from a team member who admitted that when Jack gave him advice in the past, "I almost naturally resisted, because I didn't want him to be right; I didn't want to reinforce his arrogance. So even when I knew he had a point, I just pushed it away or tried something else, because I didn't want him to feel like he was the smartest guy in the room.

"Since he's apologized, you can tell he really wants to be different. What's surprising is that I look forward to being mentored by him. I've learned way more than I thought possible. It completely flipped the switch for me because before I wouldn't have been open to his ideas or suggestions. Now, not only do I have a mentor, but I've also been learning so much because of that change in my perspective in terms of who he is and who he wants to become."

In Jack's case, it was only when he humbled himself that his employees truly began to follow him and learn from what he had to offer. He was able to acknowledge his personal limitations and faults, take responsibility for his actions, and demonstrate that he would listen to and learn from their feedback. His admission inspired his team to be more open about their individual and collective challenges and to seek out support when it was needed. Jack's story is the quintessential example of the power of humble leadership.

HUMILITY AND STRONG LEADERSHIP

In an ambitious study, SUNY Buffalo professor Bradley Owens came to three conclusions about humble leaders:

- They acknowledge their personal limits and faults while simultaneously taking responsibility for their mistakes.

- They model teachability and are exemplars of learning. They achieve this by being receptive to new ideas and devoting significant energy to listening rather than speaking. They are also very open to feedback and encourage its expression within their teams.

- They acknowledge the strengths, contributions, unique skills, and knowledge of those around them, celebrating their accomplishments so that the team member's value to the company and to the team is reinforced. In doing so, people are engaged and motivated to perform.

DEFINING HUMILITY

In an in-depth exploration aimed at classifying and measuring a number of widely valued traits, renowned positive psychologists Christopher Peterson and Martin Seligman, authors of *Character Strengths and Virtues,* posited that humility means to willingly accept new perspectives "without feeling that the self has been obliterated or damaged[80]."

Recognizing that we do not have all of the answers is a core trait of humble leadership—an approach that has been embraced in the largest and most successful organizations in the world. Lazlo Bock, former senior vice president of People Operations at Google, emphasized this important relationship in an interview with Adam Bryant of *The New York Times.*

"Without humility, you are unable to learn …" Lazlo explained. "[This makes it] really difficult to create space for other people to share their ideas[81]."

The importance of being humble is reinforced by a study conducted by Zenger Folkman that drew on 360-degree feedback data collected on more than 30,000 managers[82] [83]. "Arrogance and complacency combine in the poorest leaders as they rise, causing them to come to the dangerous conclusion that they've reached a stage in their careers where development is no longer required,"

80 Christopher Peterson and Martin E. P. Seligman, *Character Strengths and Virtues: A Handbook and Classification* (Washington: American Psychological Association, 2004).

81 Adam Bryant, "In Head-Hunting, Big Data May Not Be Such a Big Deal," *The New York Times,* June 19, 2013, https://www.nytimes.com/2013/06/20/business/in-head-hunting-big-data-may-not-be-such-a-big-deal.html.

82 Jack Zenger and Joseph Folkman, "Are You Sure You're Not a Bad Boss?" *Harvard Business Review,* August 7, 2014, https://hbr.org/2012/08/are-you-sure-youre-not-a-bad-b.

83 Data collected from approximately 300,000 of the managers' peers, direct reports, and bosses.

adding, "Closely connected to this failing is an inability to learn from mistakes, leaving these unfortunates to repeat the same ones over and over." In fact, the study authors identified "failure to improve and learn from mistakes" as one of ten fatal flaws of executives.

THE SCIENCE BEHIND "I'M SORRY"

As we learned from Jack's story, the simple act of saying "I'm sorry" can be the catalyst in strengthening or breaking a relationship.

In his bestselling book *What Got You Here Won't Get You There*, Marshall Goldsmith refers to apologizing as a "magic move."

"If a leader wants everybody else to take responsibility, the best thing they can do is to take responsibility themselves," Goldsmith explained[84] to me. "Don't blame other people. If you want everybody else to take responsibility, let them watch you do it first."

Executives who embrace apologizing are also seen as more effective. In "Leadership is a Contact Sport," a study that included more than a quarter of a million people, Goldsmith emphasized that "Leaders who discussed their own improvement priorities with their co-workers, and then regularly followed up with these co-workers, showed striking improvement[85]."

---

84   Craig Dowden, "Stop: Apologize and Listen—Understanding Behaviours to Push Us Forward," *HR Professional*, (July 2017): 29-31.
85   Marshall Goldsmith and Howard Morgan, "Leadership Is a Contact Sport: The 'Follow-up Factor' in Management Development," *Strategy Business*.

Apologizing isn't just worthwhile to the person apologizing, either. It also benefits the person to whom the apology is directed. A study published in the *Proceedings of the National Academy of Sciences* investigated how people responded to an apology from someone who had offended them[86]. The longitudinal nature of the project allowed the researchers to examine the effect of the apology on forgiveness immediately after it was given, as well as several weeks following the incident.

What they discovered was that a person was more forgiving and less angry toward their transgressor when an apology was offered, and that those feelings lasted for a considerable period of time—sometimes up to months afterwards. In fact, people appeared to forgive their transgressors in direct proportion to the extent to which apologies and other conciliatory gestures were made. If the person in error was abundantly sorry and made considerable effort to make up for the incident, the person harmed was far more likely to forgive—and to do it far more quickly—than if the person was begrudging or slow in offering an apology.

Ultimately, the researchers learned that an effective apology is invaluable in building stronger relationships and engendering trust.

86 Michael E. McCullough et al., "Reconciliation and forgiveness," *Proceedings of the National Academy of Sciences* 111, no. 30 (July 2014): 11211-11216; DOI: 10.1073/pnas.1405072111.

The Three Characteristics of an Effective Apology

Given that apologizing is a "magic move," how can we do it right? The study referenced earlier on apologizing and forgiveness sheds some light on the answer. Based on their analyses, the research team identified three characteristics of an effective apology:

1. Say "I'm Sorry."

Stating those three magic words is an important part of a successful apology. People want to hear an open acknowledgment of regret. We also need to be specific about the words or actions for which we are apologizing. Acknowledging the specific offending behaviors helps the healing process and heightens trust that this should not happen in the future because we are showing that we understand what we did wrong.

For example:

Saying, "I'm so sorry for using the last of the copy paper and forgetting to tell you that we needed to order more," is a far more effective an apology than just saying, "Sorry about that," or "Sorry, it won't happen again."

2. Offer a Form of Compensation.

This demonstrates genuine remorse for the harmful act, and an accompanied desire to facilitate healing. A direct way to do this is by asking, "What can I do to make up for this?"

It is important that the form of compensation is heartfelt and aligned with the transgression. Otherwise, the gesture can come across as not truly being an apology and instead as though we are trying to "buy them off" with a gift.

For example:

Saying, "I'm so sorry about using the last of the copy paper. I'll go buy a new box right now to replace it," is far more effective than saying, "Sorry about that. Tell you what, coffee this afternoon is on me."

This is why asking people what we can do to make amends is so critical, since the individual can provide guidance in this regard. Otherwise, a well-intentioned apologetic gesture may create even more conflict and frustration. This is especially important when we have no idea why the other person is upset with us. If we make an assumption and act accordingly, we run the risk of exacerbating the conflict.

3. Take Responsibility.

Do not attempt to justify the behaviors in any way (e.g. "I was under stress at the time" or "I know I yelled at you in front of everyone, but you just told me the project was behind"). This suggests that we are not accepting responsibility and are blaming the circumstances and/ or the other person for provoking us. This undermines trust and weakens the apology.

For example: saying, "I'm sorry, but you didn't tell me the copy paper was running low," is neither effective nor an apology.

Avoid "Non-Apologies"

Do not offer a "non-apology," either, where we apologize for offending the other person, rather than apologizing for the behavior.

An egregious example of this type of non-apology is when someone says, "I'm sorry if you took it that way." This often comes across as offensive and condescending because it can be interpreted as, "If you were smarter, you would have known what I really meant."

Lastly, and just as importantly, make it a habit of apologizing only when necessary. Overusing an apology can make it come across as a knee-jerk reaction, which can dilute its effectiveness. The more others see earnest apologizing in practice—and the more they see what high value you place on it—the more likely they are to adopt it and pass it on to others.

Mistakes are unavoidable. When they occur, we can either allow them to negatively impact how others view us, or we can use them as an opportunity to repair and strengthen relationships. The choice is ours.

THE SCIENCE OF HUMBLE LEADERSHIP

The Science of Humble Leadership

1. Better Quality Decision-Making

2. Higher Employee Engagement

3. More Effective Leadership

How can humility benefit us both as a leader and as a human being? Quite a lot, according to research:

1. Better Quality Decision-Making

Dr. Paul Nutt, professor emeritus of Management Sciences at Ohio State University's Fisher College of Business, spent over twenty years working with hundreds of companies and thousands of individuals studying the factors influencing whether a business decision turned out to be a success or failure.

He concluded that personal ego is the primary culprit in over one-third of all failed business decisions. Add to that the findings of authors David Marcum and Steven Smith, who identified that over half of all businesspeople estimate that personal egos cost their company between 6 and 15 percent of their annual revenues, and ego becomes a formidable hurdle to success[87].

To illustrate how personal ego can compromise our decision-making, Roy Baumeister, a respected social psychologist, and his colleague, Liqing Zhang, conducted a fascinating study involving the use of ego threats[88]. In one of their experiments, participants were split into two groups and each was given five dollars in quarters to play a game of chance similar to craps. Instructions for the game were identical, except that one group received the following prompt before playing:

"If you're the type of person to crack under pressure, we'd suggest you just quit right now and take your five dollars, because this game wasn't meant for you."

---

87 David Marcum and Steven Smith, *Egonomics: What Makes Ego Our Greatest Asset (or Most Expensive Liability)* (New York: Simon & Schuster, 2008).
88 Liqing Zhang, and Roy Baumeister, "Your Money or Your Self-Esteem: Threatened Egotism Promotes Costly Entrapment in Losing Endeavors," *PsycEXTRA Dataset*, 2005. doi:10.1037/e640112011-076.

Although subtle, this threat had a powerful impact. People who heard it lost significantly more money than those whose egos were not challenged in this way. The need to prove themselves often drove them to take risks that they may not have taken otherwise.

What was even more interesting was that their losses were not just limited to the financial realm—participants subjected to the ego threat also reported significantly lower self-esteem, ironically losing the very thing they were trying to recapture through their more reckless approach.

2. Higher Employee Engagement

As the leader of a talent management firm earlier in my career, my team and I conducted a survey of three hundred people in the public and private sectors to learn more about the impacts of humility on leaders as well as their teams.

Our results were compelling: employees who reported working for humble leaders were significantly happier, more productive, and experienced higher levels of job satisfaction. They also expressed a stronger desire to stay with their current employer, and they were more likely to be top performers.

> **Employees who reported working for humble leaders were significantly happier, more productive, and experienced higher levels of job satisfaction.**

Those gains were not just limited to employees: humble leaders were also rated significantly higher by their employees in terms of their effectiveness and performance. Thus, humility truly provides a win-win scenario. Benefits for the employees, the leader, and the organization abound!

In a separate study, Yi Amy Ou, assistant professor at the National University of Singapore, looked at sixty-three different companies to examine how CEO humility affected their success[89].

Her analysis revealed that humble CEOs were more likely to delegate authority and provide more autonomy to their senior management teams, which had an important trickle-down effect. As the senior leaders were given more autonomy, the layers of management underneath them were provided more of the same. The overall result was higher levels of employee engagement and performance throughout the organization.

3. More Effective Leadership

According to extensive research by Zenger Folkman, leaders who display a combination of humility, high personal standards, and a constant striving to be better, are the most effective[90].

"An aura of humility is always superior," the authors note. "Clearly it is valuable to realize that, 'While I may be good at some things, I'm probably not great at everything, and no matter how good I am, I can always get better.'"

89   Amy Y. Ou et al., "Do Humble CEOs Matter? An Examination of CEO Humility and Firm Outcomes," *Journal of Management* 44, no. 3 (2015): 1147-173, doi:10.1177/0149206315604187.
90   Jack Zenger, and Joseph Folkman, "We Like Leaders Who Underrate Themselves," *Harvard Business Review*, November 30, 2017, https://hbr.org/2015/11/we-like-leaders-who-underrate-themselves.

The Most Effective Leaders Underrate Themselves
comparing self-ratings to results from 360-degree surveys

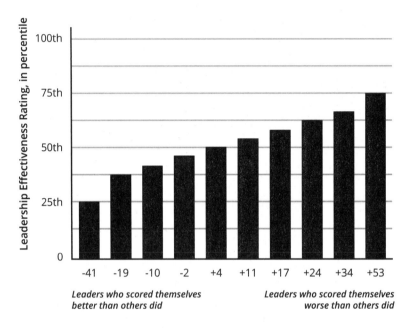

SOURCE: JACK ZENGER AND JOSEPH FOLKMAN

Jim Collins, the well-known author of the classic bestseller *Good to Great*, also reported that leader humility differentiates a great company from a good one.

Collins admits he was initially shocked to discover the strength of the association. In his book and in subsequent interviews, he explained how he made his team go back and reanalyze the data because he didn't believe humility was such an important factor. No matter how many ways they looked at it, the results were the same—humble leadership is a game changer.

PRACTICING HUMBLE LEADERSHIP

Practicing Humble Leadership

1. Take Ownership of Your Mistakes

2. Be Open to Learning and Asking Questions

3. Shine the Spotlight on Your Team

As we learned from the prevailing research, there is considerable evidence indicating humility is a vital characteristic of strong leadership. So how can we practice it?

1. Take Ownership of Our Mistakes

As discussed in the *Three Characteristics of an Effective Apology* earlier in this chapter, when people own up to their mistakes, it not only helps to strengthen that relationship; it also encourages others to follow suit.

When you make a mistake, freely admit it and take responsibility. Do this with your team, with your leaders, as well as with your customers.

Jim Whitehurst, the CEO of Red Hat (a multibillion dollar open software company) provided some great advice in this regard when I interviewed him: "People have an amazing capacity to forgive if you provide them with the opportunity."

CELEBRATE HUMILITY

Leaders are not the only ones who benefit from humility. In a recent study, researchers from Baylor University found that employees who were rated higher on honesty and humility were scored as being significantly better employees by their supervisors. "... humility and honesty not only correspond with job performance, but it predicted job performance above and beyond any of the other big five personality traits like agreeableness and conscientiousness."

These findings suggest employers receive important dividends when they keep humility and honesty top of mind when making hiring and promotion decisions. For instance, if you use psychometric assessments as part of your screening/hiring process, ensure they assess humility. You can also incorporate these questions into your employment interviews and reference checks.

Additionally, leaders can encourage humble practices on a regular basis by drawing attention to these positive behaviors when they occur. For instance, recognizing someone who acknowledged a misstep early in a project that allowed appropriate adjustments to be made could be celebrated for exemplifying this virtue. Just as we can set the example by owning up to our mistakes, leaders can encourage humility by walking the walk, and rewarding like action in others.

2. Be Open to Learning and Asking Questions

Leaders can inspire the expression of humility by recognizing and rewarding people who ask questions (e.g. delivering affirmation/ praise). Doing this highlights these behaviors as "best practices" and encourages people to follow suit in the future. We can also set the expectation that people should ask questions of each other at least as often as they advocate for their positions within team meetings. Provocative research has shown that striking this balance of inquiry versus advocacy is a key indicator of high performing teams[91].

Another effective strategy is to ask our team members for their input *before* starting a project. For example, rather than sharing our idea or strategy first, which will invariably influence the future direction, ask the team for their ideas on how to approach the work. For example, "How do you think we should tackle this assignment?" Or, before the start of a new year, ask people, "If you were in my position, what strategic priorities would you focus on?"

We can also engage our teams by informally asking questions about how we are performing as leaders. Ask "How am I doing?" to the team, fellow colleagues, as well as external stakeholders and customers. If you're concerned that people might not answer truthfully in a group setting, consider asking the question one-on-one, or use an anonymous data gathering tool (e.g. Survey Monkey) to garner honest feedback. Afterward, bring everyone together and share what you have learned and suggest that you collectively discuss how you can all be more open and honest as a group. In recognizing our desire for self-improvement, we may motivate others to do the

---

91   M. Losada and E. Heaphy, "The role of positivity and connectivity in the performance of business teams: A nonlinear dynamics model," *American Behavioral Scientist* 47, no. 6 (2004): 740-765.

same, and encourage them to feel comfortable with speaking up in case we return to a less-humble state (such as "Jack 1.0").

3. Shine the Spotlight on Your Team

By displaying humility, leaders naturally take a step back and foster more engagement by allowing their team to feel more comfortable sharing their own perspectives on issues. Ultimately, this leads their employees to be more committed to the team and to their leader. As bestselling author Adam Grant wittily surmised, "People are going to be cheering, rather than gunning for you."

There's no harm in sharing the spotlight. In fact, the better our teams perform, the more recognition we will receive because of their collective achievements.

There are numerous ways we can do this in practice. For example, rotate the chair of meetings from time to time, letting each member of the team take turns leading discussions for the day. This provides everyone an opportunity to flex their leadership muscles as well as to put their stamp on a meeting or project. Additionally, when a member of the team succeeds, make sure to promote this accomplishment both within the group, as well as throughout the organization.

If team members are subject matter experts or provide important contributions to projects, bring them along to internal senior executive meetings or to meetings with key external stakeholders and let them present their work. This provides a great learning opportunity and also allows them to receive recognition for their work.

THE HUMBLE CEO: W. BRETT WILSON AND THE HEART OF A DRAGON

W. Brett Wilson[92] is an extraordinarily successful investment banker, businessman, bestselling author, philanthropist, and former panelist on Dragon's Den, the Canadian forerunner of the TV show Shark Tank. His journey to embracing humility started when he was forced to face the man he'd become.

When we talked, he remembered the catalyzing encounter in painful detail:

"It was probably the lowest point in my life. I wanted to be at an art auction—there was a piece I really wanted to buy, but instead I was at home 'babysitting.' This is, in and of itself, pathetic, because parents don't babysit their children. They parent them. But in my mind at that time, I was babysitting.

"I decided I would participate in the auction by telephone. Early that evening the phone rang several times, but it was answered before I could get to it so I didn't pay much attention. Then I looked at my watch and realized that the piece that I was looking to buy was scheduled to have been sold already. When I called to check on it, the person on the other end of the line said, 'Brett, I called you several times and a little girl answered each time and said you were not home. It's sold. It's gone.'

"I was really upset. How could my daughter possibly have not told me that the calls were for me? I went upstairs and knocked on her door. She was lying on her bed doing homework. I was furious. She looked up at me and then crawled under the bed, afraid.

"How could you tell them I wasn't home?" I yelled.

"But, Daddy," she said. "You're never home."

---

92   Recipient of the Order of Canada, 2011; recipient of the Saskatchewan Order of Merit.

My knees melted. All of the wealth, all of the recognition—and for what? My addiction to work and the pursuit of wealth allowed me to avoid the most important areas of my life, including my family."

Brett set himself to work on addressing these personal short-comings, and sharing his story.

"In doing so, I quickly discovered how sympathetic and even empathetic friends and colleagues were to my situation—and how similar it is to their own experiences. And when I share my story with an audience of strangers, it's absolutely amazing—sometimes heart-wrenchingly emotional. I can tell by the conversations, I can tell by the tears—it resonates with them. I get feedback from business leaders saying, 'You've changed the way I look at life, the way I relate to my staff, the way I relate to my family,' or maybe the way they relate to the world of business.

"People are so worried about how others will perceive them that they are unwilling to come out from behind the mask and say, 'You know what? I screwed up. I wish I had done this differently.' That is why I started, in a very public way, to have that conversation—to say, 'Here are the mistakes I have made and here is how I live with them, and here is how I do things differently now.'

"Many business leaders don't do this because there is an under-current of shame. That doesn't need to be there. The best autobiogra-phies by business leaders share their mistakes and the lessons they've learned from them. But in order to fix these mistakes, we need to give each other room to live a more balanced life. Life is business, life is friends, life is learning, life is charity—and balancing these priorities is what makes the workplace fun."

HUMILITY ON A CORPORATE SCALE: WHEN DOMINO'S ATE HUMBLE PIE

What does humility look like on a corporate scale? Let's take a look at Domino's and the massive change it underwent in a little less than a decade.

In the mid-2000s, Domino's was really struggling. The incoming chief marketing officer, Russell Weiner, inherited flat sales cycles in the midst of a struggling economy. At the heart of Domino's' challenge was the quality of their pizzas, as various internal taste tests had highlighted. Domino's then took the extra step of gathering feedback from its various stakeholders, including customers and franchisees, to better inform their future directions. Using this critical feedback, they committed to turning out higher-quality pizza and revamped their entire recipe from crust to toppings.

Rather than try to sweep it under the rug or use creative marketing to detract attention, Domino's took the highly unusual step of tackling their shortcomings head-on. Perhaps the most forward-thinking aspect of their re-launch was a series of commercials. In these ads, customers were shown voicing their disgust at the quality of the "old recipe" pizza (e.g. "The crust tastes like cardboard"). These comments were then followed by Domino's hitting the streets with its new product to re-engage with its harshest detractors to win them back. As President Patrick Doyle noted, "You can either use negative comments to get you down or you can use them to excite you and energize your process and make a better pizza. We did the latter."

> You can either use negative comments to get you down or you can use them to excite you and energize your process.

Early returns from the campaign indicated it was an incredible success, with a 14.3 percent increase in same-store Q1 sales from 2009 to 2010, with similar gains realized in Q3 (11.2 percent improvement when compared to Q3 in 2009). This trend continued, with the stock price appreciating an astounding 2000 percent by 2017, outperforming stock stars Amazon, Apple, and even Alphabet, the parent company of Google[93].

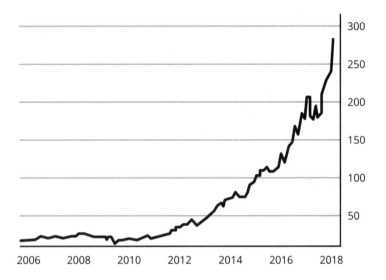

Showing vulnerability and humility goes a long way toward building a better brand and stakeholder relationships. And by demonstrating an open mind and a willingness to listen, we can turn the most ruthless critics into our staunchest supporters.

I find the Domino's example compelling because this company saved itself by being unafraid to start over. When the consumer

---

93   Yoni Blumberg, "Domino's Stock Outperformed Apple and Amazon over 7 Years-now It's the World's Largest Pizza Chain," CNBC, March 1, 2018, https://www.cnbc.com/2018/03/01/no-point-1-pizza-chain-dominos-outperformed-amazon-google-and-apple-stocks.html.

speaks, even when we may not like the message, we need to listen. Although management could have easily dismissed this feedback or decided not to reach out to their least-happy customers once they re-launched their product, Domino's included these individuals as part of their campaign with the primary aim of bringing them back into the fold. Domino's used its harshest criticism to inspire next-level greatness.

PILLAR 4

FOCUS ON THE POSITIVE

*Happiness is when what you think, what you
say, and what you do are in harmony.*

—Mahatma Gandhi

Despite his positive intentions, Robert found that he was coming across in a negative way to his team members. During his 360-degree feedback assessment, many of the statements he received read like the following:

"There's always something wrong with my ideas, so I have just stopped sharing them with him."

This was concerning. He had certainly noticed an ebb in the number of ideas his team brought to him—in fact, it was a growing point of frustration—though he had not previously considered that his approach was the reason for it. In his mind, he handled new ideas in a fair and constructive manner. So I asked him to describe a typical situation in which someone came to him with an idea.

"I listen, and then I provide some feedback on where I see gaps," he said. "This helps them avoid roadblocks before they run into them."

I told him that I understood his motivation and was not questioning his intentions. Instead, I challenged him to look at it from their perspective.

"Say you're excited about an idea and come to me with it, and I respond by saying, 'That's no good,' or even, 'That's good, but not good enough. This is how it should be done, instead.' How do you think your team members hear this?'"

A grim look crossed Robert's face. He realized that although he was trying to help, his criticism ended up demotivating his team members. Worse still, he appreciated why they stopped sharing ideas with him; it was because they were waiting for him to tell them the "right thing to do."

When I spoke with Marshall Goldsmith about this, he told me that one of the critical derailers for leaders is adding too much value; when leaders take what they receive and make it "a little better." However, according to Goldsmith, this can have two unwanted and devastating consequences:

1. While the leader may have improved the quality of the idea by 5 or 10 percent, the team member's commitment and engagement to executing the idea drops by half or more because he or she no longer feels ownership of it.

2. Team members become less willing to share ideas because whatever they propose will "not be good enough."

As Robert and I continued our conversation, we explored a different way he could react to this situation in the future. In particular, I asked him to reflect on what is gained by critiquing their ideas. If Robert did not say anything, for instance, would the organization, the team, or the individual be exposed to any strategic or critical risk? Said another way, is the critique more stylistic than imperative? If the former, it is better not to say anything.

When people are excited about an idea, it can be tremendously disheartening to hear about what is wrong with it before they even start. The best approach a leader can take is to share in their enthusiasm and simply ask a few insightful questions to help guide their thinking.

When leaders do have concerns, they can make them more constructive by asking questions rather than making statements. For example, if you are worried about the budgetary implications of a particular project, rather than saying, "I don't have the budget for that," ask a question to your employee such as, "How do you see this fitting into our current budget?"

Robert agreed to implement this approach. In a follow-up survey, the results suggested that his team felt the environment was far more positive and encouraging than it had been before. Importantly, they reported more freedom to express their ideas and take creative risks. They also commented that they felt significantly more ownership for their work, were more committed to following through, and were learning more as a consequence.

POSITIVE LEADER, POSITIVE PEOPLE

In a study of US Navy teams on connectivity and the importance of positivity, it was noted that "In environments thought to be even more stoic than corporate

America—like the military—leaders who openly express their positivity get the most out of their teams[94]. In the US Navy, researchers found, annual prizes for efficiency and preparedness are far more frequently awarded to squadrons whose commanding officers are openly encouraging. On the other hand, the squadrons receiving the lowest marks in performance are generally led by commanders with a negative, controlling, and aloof demeanor. Even in an environment where one would think the harsh 'military taskmaster' style of leadership would be most effective, positivity wins out."

DEFINING FOCUS ON THE POSITIVE

Focusing on the positive is not an all-or-none proposition—it is not about eliminating the negative altogether. Instead, it is deciding where we are going to invest the majority of our energy and attention. Based on the research to date, how we answer this question may have an enormous impact on our success and the success of our team/organization.

According to positive psychologist Barbara L. Fredrickson, when we are in a positive state of mind, we are much more innovative, more creative, and more willing to take risks. We see the world as filled with opportunity rather than threat, and we are more engaged and more likely to take action as a result. We also experience and

---

94   W. Bachman, "Nice Guys Finish First: A SYMLOG Analysis of U.S. Naval Commands," in Polley, R.B. et al. (Eds.), *The SYMLOG practitioner: Applications of small group research* (New York: Praeger, 1988).

benefit from a subset of positive emotions, including joy, interest, contentment, and love.

Conversely, when we are in a negative mindset, we become much more protective and risk-averse. We are afraid of what we could lose, so we rarely step out of our comfort zone and strongly resist change.

She has termed this the "broaden and build" theory[95].

Positive emotions, she explains, broaden an individual's inclination to act: joy sparks the desire to play, interest encourages one to explore, contentment provokes us to savor the moment, and love provides a safe environment in which these expressions can occur. Consequently, these emotions promote the discovery of ideas, social bonds, and novel and creative actions that build that person's physical, intellectual, social, and psychological resources.

"Importantly," she adds, "these resources function as reserves that can be drawn on later to improve the odds of successful coping."

This theory goes a long way in explaining why adaptability is such a key element of a company's survival today; the ones that have a positive outlook and are able to pivot quickly are more resilient and, as a result, more successful.

THE SCIENCE OF FOCUSING ON THE POSITIVE

The Science of Focusing on the Positive

1. Improved Physical Health

2. Greater Creativity

3. Positive Group Attitude (Emotional Contagion)

---

95   Barbara L. Fredrickson, "Broaden-And-Build Theory of Positive Emotions," *Encyclopedia of Social Psychology*, doi:10.4135/9781412956253.n75.

Beyond resiliency and adaptability, focusing on the positive has an impact on practically every aspect of business (and life, for that matter).

1. Improved Physical Health

In 1998, Carnegie Mellon professor Sheldon Cohen and his colleagues conducted a fascinating study into the links between happiness and physical health[96]. Participants were first evaluated for their general levels of health and happiness before being sequestered in a quarantined facility and exposed to a nasally administered cold virus.

Over the course of five days, participants ate the same foods, followed the same routines, and lived in the same environment. At the end of the study, of those participants who contracted the virus, those who were initially rated as "happier" reported not being as sick as their less happy counterparts.

While some may assume that this was only because the happier participants chose to take a more pleasant and perhaps naïve view of the situation, the physicians actually explored this disparity. Interestingly, the happier people not only reported feeling less sick, they also displayed fewer objective indicators of sickness. They had less sneezing, less mucous, and lower temperatures.

This influence of happiness on health was the subject of a literature review conducted by psychologist Ed Diener, who earned the nickname "Dr. Happiness" due to his twenty-five-plus years of research into the area[97].

---

96 Jane E. Brody, "A Cold Fact: High Stress Can Make You Sick," *The New York Times*, May 12, 1998, https://archive.nytimes.com/www.nytimes.com/specials/women/warchive/980512_940.html.
97 Diener, Oishi, and Lucas (2017) define "subjective well-being" as how individuals evaluate or appraise their own lives.

After reviewing more than one hundred fifty studies, Diener and his colleagues concluded that happiness impacts our health in a variety of areas including cardiovascular and immune system functioning, the speed with which wounds heal, and the lowering of inflammation.

Some research has even suggested that happiness leads to a longer life.

In evaluating the autobiographical essays of some 670 Catholic nuns, researchers discovered that those who expressed greater positivity at the time of the writing (the essays were written when the nuns took their vows, typically in their early twenties) lived significantly longer—in some cases, up to ten years longer—than those who wrote with a less positive leaning.

The link between happiness and physical health is so strong that Diener recommends that during our annual physical examination, one of the first things a doctor should ask is "How happy are you?" because it is just as important as our weight, diet, exercise, and smoking habits.

His calls have not gone unnoticed: "We in the health care professions need to notice and inquire about happiness the same way we do other aspects of our patients' lives," writes Dr. Danielle Ofri in a *New York Times* Op-Ed[98]. "The association of happiness and health remains a potent touchstone in both popular and medical culture …. How a person is feeling emotionally needs to be acknowledged and explored."

Gallup reached similar conclusions while conducting research for its Well-Being Index. On average, it found that unhappy employees took significantly more sick days, staying home an average of 1.25

98   Danielle Ofri, "Why Doctors Care About Happiness," *The New York Times*, March 3, 2016, https://well.blogs.nytimes.com/2016/03/03/why-doctors-care-about-happiness.

days more per month than their happier counterparts, which trans-lates to an additional fifteen sick days per year.

2. Greater Creativity

Happy doctors, it turns out, also tend to be more creative, and when they are more creative, they are more likely to make more accurate diagnoses.

In exploring how mood impacts physicians' performance, a study uncovered how positive affect counteracts the issue of "anchoring," a psychological term referring to the difficulty involved in letting go of an initial judgment, even when new information comes to the surface[99]. All human beings experience this phenomenon and it is particularly challenging for doctors, who need to remain open to new information in order to reach a proper diagnosis.

Researchers began by dividing doctors into three groups, one of which was primed to feel happy by giving each participant a piece of candy (which they could not eat until after the study concluded to avoid any influence the sugar rush may have on results). The second group was given neutral, medical-related statements to review, and the third group was a control. Each of the doctors was then given a file to diagnose.

Surprisingly, the positive-primed doctors not only reached the correct diagnosis nearly twice as fast as the control group, they also displayed two-and-a-half times less anchoring and exhibited signifi-cantly more creativity than either group.

99   Carlos A. Estrada et al., "Positive Affect Facilitates Integration of Information and Decreases Anchoring in Reasoning among Physicians," *Egyptian Journal of Medical Human Genetics*, May 25, 2002, https://www.sciencedirect.com/science/article/pii/S0749597897927345.

3. Positive Group Attitude (Emotional Contagion)

In exploring how our emotions interact on a societal level, researcher Sigal Barsade observed that "emotions, both positive and negative, actually spread among your employees like viruses."

As part of her investigation, Barsade had participants take turns role-playing a department head advocating for a merit-based raise for an employee to the rest of the group, which comprised the "salary committee[100]." The committee then negotiated a raise based on a set amount of available funds and the overall benefit to the company.

"Emotions, both positive and negative, actually spread among your employees like viruses."

What the participants didn't know was that an actor was seeded in each group who was trained to portray one of four distinct moods: cheerful enthusiasm, serene warmth, hostile irritability, or depressed sluggishness.

It turned out that the groups in which the two positive emotions were spread not only experienced an increase in positive mood, "these groups also displayed more cooperation, less interpersonal conflict, and felt they'd performed better on their task than groups in which negative emotions were spread." Additionally, "Groups in which people felt positive emotions actually made decisions that allocated the available money more equitably."

---

100 Sigale Barsade, "Faster than a Speeding Text: 'Emotional Contagion' At Work," Psychology Today, October 15, 2014, https://www.psychologytoday.com/us/blog/the-science-work/201410/faster-speeding-text-emotional-contagion-work.

OVERCOMING NEGATIVE STIMULI

In a review of more than thirty years of social science research on the topic of positive versus negative stimuli, Roy Baumeister and his team at Case Western Reserve University came to the conclusion that "bad is stronger than good[101]." That is, "bad emotions, bad parents, and bad feedback have more impact than good ones, and bad information is processed more thoroughly than good."

With far more positive energy needed to outweigh the negative, then, we should be prepared to balance feedback proportionally, reframing setbacks so as to focus on failure less and more on the small wins that come out of it.

This is the basic premise behind the Progress Principle, which was proposed by Teresa Amabile and Steven Kramer in their book by the same name. In exploring the triggers behind people's "best day" and "worst day" at work, they discovered that, "Of all the things that can boost emotions, motivation, and perceptions during a workday, the single most important is making progress in meaningful work[102]." On the best days, the researchers observed, people typically made

---

101 Roy F. Baumeister et al., "Bad is Stronger Than Good," *Review of General Psychology* 5, no. 4, 323-370, DOI: 10.1037//1089-2680.5.4.323.
102 With meaningful work being described as goals that can be either lofty or modest, as long as they have meaning to the worker.

progress in their meaningful work, and on worst days, they often experienced setbacks[103].

"If you are a manager, the Progress Principle holds clear implications for where to focus your efforts," Amabile states. "It suggests that you have more influence than you may realize over employees' well-being, motivation, and creative output."

That is, "by supporting people and their daily progress in meaningful work, managers improve not only the inner work lives of their employees but also the organization's long-term performance, which enhances inner work life even more."

PRACTICE FOCUSING ON THE POSITIVE

Practice Focusing on the Positive

1. When Giving Praise, Make it Descriptive Rather Than Evaluative

2. See the Opportunity in Failure

3. Focus on Strengths

How, then, can one leverage the benefits of focusing on the positive?

---

103 Teresa Amabile and Steven J. Kramer, "The Power of Small Wins," *Harvard Business Review,* June 8, 2016, https://hbr.org/2011/05/the-power-of-small-wins.

1. When Giving Praise, Make it Descriptive Rather Than Evaluative

Although saying "good job" or "fabulous idea" can make someone feel good temporarily, it offers no direction for the future. In some cases it may even be taken the wrong way—as a brush off or as false praise—if the recipient lacks trust in the feedback provider. Additionally, non-specific, evaluative praise does not encourage growth; it simply states an opinion at the time.

Instead, leaders benefit more from focusing on and recognizing specific praiseworthy actions. For instance, instead of saying "Great work out there," replace with, "Those statistics you shared added a lot of value and you made your points very clearly. As a result, everyone was listening intently to your presentation this morning." Not only does this acknowledge the presenter for a job well done and offer valued praise, it also provides guidance as to what was done well and what should be continued in the future.

WHO IS YOUR "BEST REFLECTED SELF?"

A positive psychology exercise that can be adapted to the workplace to highlight talent and enhance happiness is called the "Best Reflected Self". Traditionally, individuals ask friends, family members, and work colleagues to write a detailed story outlining when and where the individual was operating at his or her best. It would be a situation in which the person seemed fully in the zone and was flourishing. Research has demonstrated this is a very powerful exercise that leads to higher well-being and resilience.

Leaders can modify this practice within their own teams. Specifically, the leader could either ask each team member to write a "story" (a couple of sentences to a paragraph or two is adequate) about each of their colleagues in terms of when they saw him or her at their best. For instance, a "Best Reflected Self" story could simply state, "You have an amazing talent for taking complex ideas and expressing them simply, such as you did with Client X's spreadsheet request. The concept was incredibly clear and the information conveyed concisely. It was easy for everyone to follow. You turned an abstract and challenging concept into something actionable that benefitted everyone involved."

These stories provide tremendous insight into the strengths each individual brings to the team, and it also enables the team to express appreciation to one another. As noted in the self-awareness chapter, this type of recognition and acknowledgement is sorely lacking within organizations today.

2. See the Opportunity in Failure

Generally, failure is viewed as something to avoid at all costs, yet when considered from an Edisonian "now we know what doesn't work" perspective, failure becomes a positive learning opportunity.

According to Jim Estill, CEO of Danby Appliances, a manufacturer and distributor of household appliances, failure is a critical part of success. As he explained to me, "Having a failure does not make me a failure. In fact, I want to have a culture of accepting failure because if we don't have any failures, we're not trying hard enough[104]."

Consider Eli Lilly & Co., one of the top drug companies in the world, which encourages its scientists to accept that failure will happen.

In practice, experimental drugs have a 90 percent failure rate[105]. Rather than scratching those projects, Eli Lilly looks into other potential uses for the compounds, going so far as to have a dedicated team whose job it is to conduct deep retrospective analyses of the drugs' failure points. This approach has resulted in a number of drugs found to be successful in combating ailments that they were not originally created to treat. For instance, Eli Lilly's experimental chemotherapy drug Almita was almost abandoned before its team conducted a failure review, during which researchers identified how the potentially tumor-reducing compound could be used to combat mesothelioma.

Other companies have found their own ways to celebrate the benefits of learning from failure, from Tata's "Dare to Try" award to Proctor & Gamble's "Heroic Failure Award[106]." At the annual Tata Group Innovation Forum, for instance, InnoVista awards are given for Promising Innovations, Design Honors, and Leading-Edge Proven Technologies, yet the most popular is typically the Forum's "Dare

104 Craig Dowden, "A CEO's Lessons on Learning, Losing and Lasting," *Financial Post*, June 26, 2017, https://business.financialpost.com/executive/a-ceos-lessons-on-learning-losing-and-lasting.

105 Thomas M. Burton, "By Learning From Failures, Lilly Keeps Drug Pipeline Full," *The Wall Street Journal*, April 21, 2004, https://www.wsj.com/articles/SB108249266648388235.

106 Jacob Morgan, "Why Failure Is The Best Competitive Advantage," *Forbes*, March 30, 2015, https://www.forbes.com/sites/jacobmorgan/2015/03/30/why-failure-is-the-best-competitive-advantage/#538e3e1759df.

to Try" category, which "recognizes and rewards novel, daring, and seriously attempted ideas that did not achieve the desired results[107]."

As we see with Tata and the growing number of companies embracing this concept, rewarding failure encourages innovation and allows teams to remove inefficiencies as they hone in on success.

> **F.A.I.L.**
> Despite the emotional weight carried by the word "fail," several clever acronyms have been created to reduce the stigma attached to it:
>
> | First | From |
> |-------|------|
> | Attempt | Action |
> | In | I |
> | Learning | Learn |

DON'T BE PARANOID; EMBRACE PRONOIA

I am a kind of paranoid in reverse. I suspect people of plotting to make me happy.

—Seymour Glass in *Raise High the Roof Beam, Carpenters*, by J.D. Salinger

Drawing from research conducted by Fred Goldner in the early 1980s, psychologist Dr. Brian Little describes pronoia as "the delusional belief that other people are plotting your well-being or saying good things about you behind your back."

---

107 Amrita Nair Ghaswalla, "Daring to Fail: A Programme That Lauds the Unsuccessful," *Business Line*, September 24, 2014, https://www.thehindubusinessline.com/companies/Daring-to-fail-a-programme-that-lauds-the-unsuccessful/article20872449.ece.

This mind-set, Dr. Little explains, is the product of both nature and nurture, or, as he describes them, biogenic and sociogenic forces. Some people are more naturally inclined toward this positive way of thinking, while others need to learn it.

In a 2015 review of the pronoia literature, Dr. Leon Seltzer writes that "Pronoia depicts not a disposition of social apprehensiveness and skepticism, but a far more welcoming orientation: one characterized by feelings of hope, trust, faith, and love[108]. And these much more positively regarded qualities are themselves related to a strong inclination toward optimism and resilience."

To become "pronoid," we need to cultivate a perception that the world is less out to "get us" and more inclined to help us. When embraced on a deeper level, this attitude can boost self-confidence and increase the likelihood that we will recognize opportunities that we may have missed with a more negative mind-set.

3. Focus on Strengths

Leveraging the power of strengths is an idea that has been keenly developed by the Gallup organization, which has documented myriad benefits of this approach. In one large-scale study, people who were

---

108 Leon F. Seltzer, "Might You Suffer from Reverse Paranoia?" Psychology Today, December 2, 2015, https://www.psychologytoday.com/us/blog/evolution-the-self/201512/might-you-suffer-reverse-paranoia.

aware of their strengths and utilized them more frequently in the workplace were significantly more likely to be top performers[109].

The benefits of using our strengths are not just limited to performance. Further research by Gallup shows that employees who were given "strengths feedback" had a 14.9 percent lower turnover rate than employees who did not receive such feedback[110]. The value of strengths-based feedback extends to teams as well. A one-hour coaching session geared toward understanding and applying their strengths resulted in an increased engagement score compared to counterparts who did not take part in such a discussion. Furthermore, those gains had a cascading effect, increasing the overall engagement score of the team following the intervention. This indicates the positive and contagious impacts that can be realized by focusing on our strengths.

Leaders can successfully leverage a strengths-based approach with the following steps:

A. Develop Awareness

Being aware of our personal strengths makes intuitive sense—how can we maximize our time using our strengths if we do not even know what they are?

Several assessment tools exist that provide detailed insight into our strengths. Perhaps the most well-known is Gallup's Strengths-Finder 2.0, which yields a personalized report detailing the individual's five signature strengths and shares customized tips for activities/opportunities to leverage these strengths within the workplace.

---

109 Peter Flade et al., "Employees Who Use Their Strengths Outperform Those Who Don't," Gallup, October 8, 2015, https://news.gallup.com/businessjournal/186044/employees-strengths-outperform-don.aspx.

110 Kim Asplund and Nikki Blacksmith, "The Secret of Higher Performance," Gallup, May 3, 2011, https://news.gallup.com/businessjournal/147383/secret-higher-performance.aspx.

Although lacking the rigor of an assessment tool, another option for developing strengths awareness is to encourage employees to obtain feedback on their strengths from colleagues and friends; making sure employees ask for specific feedback and examples, wherever possible. For instance, when exploring what others think of their interpersonal skills, team members could ask, "How well would you say I listen to others? Can you give me some recent examples?" The clearer the feedback, the more likely your employees will be able to take action on it.

TEAM-BASED EXERCISE: STRENGTH BUILDING

Dr. Kim Cameron, co-founder of the Center for Positive Organizations at the University of Michigan, created an excellent strengths-based exercise for teams. Here's how it works:

Give each member of your team a set of blank index cards that totals the number of people on your team minus one. If the group has ten people, for example, each person should have nine cards.

Then, the person writes a different name in the upper right-hand corner of each card, such that there is one card per team member. On one side of each card, have the employee write down the strengths of the individual named on the card. Then on the back, have the employee write down all of the strengths the named person possesses that are unrealized—the ones that he or she may not even see and could start using right away.

Once filled out, each person in the group collects their cards and writes two paragraphs—one being a summary of what they learned about their observed strengths, and the other about how they could be contributing through their unrealized strengths.

Have everyone come back together and share their two paragraphs with the group and have each team member commit to using their strengths to the betterment of the team. It's a very powerful and motivating exercise.

B. Have a Strengths Discussion

Once employees are made aware of their strengths, leaders should follow up with one-on-one discussions with each of their team members. It is important that the leader not take control of the conversation. One very effective way to ensure this happens is for the leader to ask questions rather than provide observations. These questions could include:

- Do you feel as though you are applying your strengths on a regular basis?

- How do you think you can leverage your talents more in your current role?

- Are there other projects within the organization that could utilize your talents?

C. Assign Tasks Based on Strengths

With a greater understanding of the strengths profile of their group, leaders can work with employees to determine where their talents best fit the team requirements, bringing maximum capacity to initiatives rather than just assigning tasks randomly or through another self-directed process. For instance, a leader could create a spreadsheet mapping out all of their team's individual strengths so the group could quickly and easily identify where their team is strongest and where it is lacking. A team may have a wealth of creatives with high-level ideas, for example, but a lack of detail-oriented individuals to make sure those concepts are properly implemented.

Maximizing opportunities to use our strengths is critical to realizing the goal of "being one's best." This is a shared responsibility in which each of us can play a role. Celebrating and capitalizing on our talents benefits all parties and contributes toward building a culture where "loving your job" is more than a dream; it is a reality.

> Celebrating and capitalizing on our talents benefits all parties and contributes toward building a culture where "loving your job" is more than a dream; it is a reality.

A CEO WHO FOCUSES ON THE POSITIVE: TONY HSIEH

When Amazon founder Jeff Bezos talks about the roughly $1 billion acquisition of online shoe company Zappos, he often notes that it was as much a cultural acquisition as it was a business one.

For years, Zappos was continually rated by *Fortune* magazine as one of the top companies to work for[111]. They outranked multiple luxury big name brands such as Jaguar and Ritz-Carlton, and they did it despite the fact that they are a call center—an environment that is

---

111 Kacy Burdette, "Zappos.com," *Fortune*, March 10, 2015, http://fortune.com/best-companies/2015/zappos-com-86/.

generally rated as one of the most challenging in which to work and also tends to have the highest disengagement scores.

How did they achieve this? In his book, *Delivering Happiness*, Zappos CEO Tony Hsieh states that from the day he bought the company, his goal was to create a culture where people wanted to be happy. In encouraging his employees to embrace their own uniqueness, he also drove home the importance of how everything that was done or said in the organization needed to focus on building a positive experience—for the employees as well as for the customers. "At the end of the day," wrote Hsieh, "it's not what you say or what you do, but how you make people feel that matters the most."

The following are some ways that this pioneer online shoe company does things a little differently:

1. **Interview process.** When a candidate is selected for an interview, rather than follow the standard process, Zappos recruiters engage in a "cultural interview." For example, interviewers ask potential candidates to rate their level of weirdness on a scale of one to ten. Individuals who provide a very low number are screened out, as they are seen as too conservative. Another popular question is, "What was the title of your last position and was it appropriate?" This is designed to test for the degree of humility in the candidate. If they are self-aggrandizing in their response, they are not a good fit.

2. **Onboarding Process.** After passing the interview, candidates receive two weeks of classroom training, which includes a detailed introduction to the "Zappos Way." An interesting twist is that following the training, the company offers these same employees $2,000 to quit. This is a strategic investment, as it weeds out employees who do not identify

with or fit the culture. Most importantly, those who turn down the money make a powerful public statement about their commitment to Zappos. In the long run, it is much cheaper to pay a candidate $2,000 to leave than to replace an employee who is not committed to stay.

3. **Commitment to Learning**. Tony Hsieh has been instrumental in driving curriculum development for the entire organization. Employees are fully paid for their participation and the training occurs during regular work hours. Hsieh's ultimate goal is to have all new recruits ready for senior leadership positions within five to seven years.

4. **Creating a Culture Book**. Each year, employees contribute unedited stories and observations about what it means to be a part of Zappos. Experts agree that culture provides direction on what behaviors are—and are not—appropriate in the day-to-day workings of an organization. There is nothing more powerful in expressing what it is like within a company than having employees literally write the book on it.

5. **Playing**. Managers are required to spend at least 10 to 20 percent of their time "goofing off" with their team to help enhance and maintain morale.

Although not all of Hsieh's ideas may apply to every organization, reflecting on the underlying values within each of his strategies provides insight into possible concrete action steps that can be taken to create a culture based on delivering happiness.

FOCUS ON THE POSITIVE ON A CORPORATE SCALE: JETBLUE

While Southwest Airlines is consistently touted as the top US carrier, there's another airline that flies close behind[112]. In fact, it has previously taken the top spot as the best low-cost airline, and when Southwest unseats it in the J.D. Power rankings for Best North American Airline, it is usually only by a few points.

Throughout its existence, JetBlue has based every major decision on its founding mission: to bring humanity back to air travel. This means focusing on a positive customer experience in all aspects, from comfort to connectivity to entertainment. They also believe strongly in having a positive impact on the world through charitable giving, such as when it launched a hurricane relief program for Puerto Rico following Hurricane Maria. As the largest air carrier in San Juan, JetBlue president Robin Hayes stated that in "Using our strengths as an airline, our partnerships, and our mission of inspiring humanity, we aim to make a positive impact on this island we call home[113]." To that effect, the airline began offering free flights to emergency personnel, military, and volunteers, and pledged to match relief donations through their GlobalGiving campaign of up to half a million dollars[114].

Additionally, JetBlue has been cited as a "rare example" of an organization that focuses on positive feedback, asking its customers, "If you have something nice to say, by all means—say it[115]!"

112 Benjamin Mutzabaugh, "J.D. Power: Alaska Air, Southwest Are (again) the USA's Best Airlines for 2018," *USA Today*, May 30, 2018, https://www.usatoday.com/story/travel/flights/todayinthesky/2018/05/30/j-d-power-alaska-air-southwest-jetblue-best-airlines/652569002/.

113 Bridget Hallinan, "JetBlue Launches Hurricane Relief Plan for Puerto Rico," *Condé Nast Traveler*, September 28, 2017, https://www.cntraveler.com/story/jetblue-launches-hurricane-relief-plan-for-puerto-rico.

114 "JetBlue Airways," GlobalGiving, https://www.globalgiving.org/jetblue/.

115 "JetBlue | Share a Compliment," JetBlue | Our Planes, https://www.jetblue.com/contact-us/email/compliment/.

This positive perspective, of asking customers what went right instead of what went wrong, was the core focus of a series of studies led by associate marketing professor at Utah State's Huntsman School of Business, Sterling Bone.

In a longitudinal field study conducted with two established national companies, Bone and his colleagues discovered that using positive language at significant points in the sales process, from solicitation to requesting feedback about the purchase experience, can positively influence a customer's perception of the experience.

Combined, the studies indicate that companies should focus on positive language as part of the customer feedback experience[116]. In fact, by simply giving the language a more positive focus, the researchers discovered a "32.88 percent increase in customer spending relative to a survey with no open-ended positive solicitation."

Similar to the findings and recommendations of this study, JetBlue also takes an "overly friendly approach to customer service" in a proactive effort to prevent escalations, encouraging employees to focus on being sympathetic and caring, resulting in its flight attendants and even pilots being celebrated as "caring, spontaneous, and personable" in an otherwise "cold and seemingly heartless industry[117]."

Consequently, even though the airline is less than half the size of competitors Southwest, Delta, and United, JetBlue boasts some of the most loyal customers in the industry[118, 119].

116 Sterling A. Bone et al., "Mere Measurement Plus: How Solicitation of Open-Ended Positive Feedback Influences Customer Purchase Behavior," *Journal of Marketing Research* 54, no. 1 (February 2017): 156-170.
117 "JetBlue Leads The Way In February," SeekingAlpha, March 15, 2018, https://seekingalpha.com/article/4156677-jetblue-leads-way-february.
118 Ibid.
119 Sean Williams, "The Surprising Airline That's Now Leading in Customer Loyalty," The Motley Fool, February 28, 2016, https://www.fool.com/investing/general/2016/02/28/surprising-airline-now-leading-in-customer-loyalty.aspx.

PILLAR 5

MEANING AND PURPOSE

Purpose provides activation energy for living.

—Dr. Mihaly Csikszentmihalyi

One can quickly lose their sense of purpose when the onslaught of everyday tasks feels overwhelming. This was exactly the situation that Laura was facing. After several years as the director of a long-term patient care facility, she was reaching burnout, despite her deep intrinsic desire to help the people she served.

Through our coaching discussions, we discovered that her most meaningful activity was saying hello and spending time with the residents. Unfortunately, because of the volume of work she navigated every day, she felt she rarely, if ever, had time to engage in casual conversation. So the question became, "How can we create that time?"

"Right now," I asked her, "what's the maximum amount of time you can commit to this activity per day?"

After a few minutes of reflection, she said, "I think the most I can do is fifteen minutes, but I don't even think that's possible."

As with most things in life, if we do not schedule time for it, it does not happen, so she committed to setting aside fifteen minutes on her calendar each day to engage in this activity. We also agreed that she would not cancel this meeting unless absolutely necessary (e.g., emergency), regardless of what was happening. This ensured nothing interfered with this critical task.

When we met again two weeks later, she was thrilled. Those fifteen minutes she spent each day walking the floor and saying hi to the residents was a motivational shot in the arm. She felt more productive, engaged, and happier than she had for a long, long time. Additionally, although she initially believed she did not have the time to spare, she admitted that on some days she was able to dedicate as much as thirty minutes for this activity, and was restructuring her day to increase that time across the board: a perfect example of the motivational power of meaning.

DEFINING MEANING AND PURPOSE

What is the "why" behind your work? This is something above and beyond your paycheck. At its core, meaning is what gets you out of bed in the morning.

In plain terms, "purpose" is the reason that something is done. The purpose of a car is transportation, while the purpose of a lamp is to create light. "Meaning" comes from ascribing a greater value to that purpose. A car can have greater meaning to you because it is a lovingly restored antique; the lamp because it is your favorite one to read by. When the *purpose* of a company is one that we value greatly, such as helping others, then its purpose has greater *meaning*.

An excellent example of a company with meaningful purpose is Bombas, which *Forbes* describes as a "social impact sock company[120]."

When co-founder David Heath read that socks were the number one most requested clothing item in homeless shelters, he and his colleague Randy Goldberg developed the idea for a sock company focused on quality and affordability that would donate a pair of socks to those in need for every pair they sold.

Launched in August 2013, Heath and Goldberg's initial goal was to give away one million socks by 2025. As of 2018, they had far exceeded that number, with ten million socks donated.

"Every time we volunteer and interact with the community we serve, I am more and more inspired to succeed," Heath says[121]. "Since day one, volunteering with the homeless and in-need communities has been engraved in Bombas and our culture."

This is a purpose that the company's small yet busy team is proud to get behind. At its four-year mark, Bombas has a remarkably low turnover rate (4 percent), which its co-founder attributed directly to their culture[122].

120 Tori Utley, "Meet Bombas, The Social Impact Company That Gave 2 Million Pairs Of Socks To The Homeless," *Forbes*, November 23, 2017, https://www.forbes.com/sites/toriutley/2017/02/06/meet-bombas-the-social-impact-company-that-gave-2-million-pairs-of-socks-to-the-homeless/#58948d2b288b.

121 Jonathan Wasserstrum, "The Founder Questionnaire: David Heath, Co-Founder & CEO of Bombas," *Forbes*, August 23, 2017, https://www.forbes.com/sites/leewasserstrum/2017/08/22/the-founder-questionnaire-david-health-co-founder-ceo-of-bombas/#3db26f772852.

122 Paul Sullivan, "When Office Meetings Leave the Office Behind," *The New York Times*, September 1, 2017, https://www.nytimes.com/2017/09/01/your-money/unusual-office-meetings.html.

"No matter what happens in your business," says Goldberg, "don't sacrifice the impact you're making—it has to stay the primary driver[123]."

THE SCIENCE OF MEANING AND PURPOSE

The Science of Meaning and Purpose

1. Higher Job Satisfaction/Well-Being

2. Increased Engagement

3. Better Performance

4. Greater Motivation

When looking for a job, research shows we value "a sense of purpose" above income, job security, hours, work-life balance, and even the opportunity for promotion[124].

A review of more than forty years of research revealed that the greatest indicator for achieving purpose is when a job allows us to have "a positive impact on other people[125]."

There's a well-known story about President Kennedy and his brief, yet powerful exchange with a janitor at NASA in the early 1960s. During his visit to the space station, the president happened

123 Tori Utley, "Meet Bombas, The Social Impact Company That Gave 2 Million Pairs Of Socks To The Homeless," *Forbes*, November 23, 2017, https://www.forbes.com/sites/toriutley/2017/02/06/meet-bombas-the-social-impact-company-that-gave-2-million-pairs-of-socks-to-the-homeless/#58948d2b288b.
124 Adam Grant, "How Customers Can Rally Your Troops," *Harvard Business Review*, August 1, 2014, https://hbr.org/2011/06/how-customers-can-rally-your-troops.
125 Adam Grant, "The #1 Feature of a Meaningless Job," LinkedIn, January 29, 2014, https://www.linkedin.com/pulse/20140129133724-69244073-the-1-feature-of-a-meaningless-job/.

to ask the gentleman what he did there, and the janitor replied, "Mr. President, I am putting a man on the moon."

When people believe that their jobs contribute to something bigger than themselves, the benefits to both the individual as well as to their organization abound.

1. Higher Job Satisfaction/Well-Being

In a fascinating study involving college students and their post-graduation goals, Christopher Niemiec, Edward Deci, and Richard Ryan discovered that students who reported having intrinsic, meaningful aspirations prior to graduation, such as personal growth or community involvement, had higher levels of job satisfaction and subjective well-being when evaluated one year later[126].

On the other hand, students who were driven by more extrinsic goals, such as pursuing money or recognition, reported little impact on their sense of well-being. In fact, the extrinsically motivated students often showed increased anxiety, depression, and other indicators of poor well-being, even when they attained their goals.

2. Increased Engagement

In investigating what influences job satisfaction, Dr. Amy Wrzesniewski, Professor of Organizational Behavior at the Yale School of Management, collaborated with colleagues to identify three "work orientations" that identify the meaning employees assign to their work.

---

126 Christopher P. Niemiec et al., "The Path Taken: Consequences of Attaining Intrinsic and Extrinsic Aspirations in Post-College Life," *Journal of Research in Personality* 73, no. 3 (2009): 291–306.

- **Jobs**, Wrzesniewski explains, are done for the paycheck[127]. They are typically approached as a nine-to-five endeavor and are viewed solely as a means to an end. Nothing more.

- Those who view their work as a **career** are more interested in advancement, rather than being excited about the particular area in which they work. As long as they feel they are progressing, they are fulfilled.

- Lastly, those who see their work as a **calling** believe that they are doing what they were born to do. Even if they woke up the next morning and won the lottery, they would still be excited to keep working.

Based on her initial research, she found that those who describe their work as a "calling" were more likely to find greater meaning, and be more engaged, in what they do.

During my first stint as the managing director of a talent management firm, our team decided to look into how Wrzesniewski's work orientations impacted employees. Our results were striking. Individuals who saw their work as a calling were significantly more engaged and happier in their work than their counterparts who viewed their work as a job or career. For instance, 77 percent of people who saw their work as a **calling** reported feeling always engaged in their work. Conversely, none of those who viewed their work as a **job** reported feeling this way.

127 Katherine Brooks, "Job, Career, Calling: Key to Happiness and Meaning at Work?" Psychology Today, June 29, 2012, https://www.psychologytoday.com/us/blog/career-transitions/201206/job-career-calling-key-happiness-and-meaning-work.

3. Better Performance

When a university asked Adam Grant to help with the high turnover rate at the call center for their alumni scholarship program, he agreed—on the condition that he could conduct an experiment[128].

By their very nature, call centers are challenging places to work. Employees have low autonomy (they are required to read scripts word-for-word) and high pressure (high focus on "sales"), and even though their purpose in this case was a positive one—to solicit donations from alumni for the school's scholarship fund—employees still suffered from very low engagement. The rejection rate for these calls was around 99 percent and the annual turnover approximately 400 percent, meaning that every three months their staff complement was entirely different. Despite the administration's best efforts to incentivize staff with perks such as pizza parties and stress management seminars, nothing was working.

To start, Grant ingeniously divided the call center agents into three groups—"personal benefit," "task significance," and "control"—with nobody allowed to share what was happening in their group until the experiment was over.

In the control group, nothing was done. Their performance over the subsequent month was simply evaluated with no intervention to provide a baseline for the other two groups.

In the personal benefit group, the call center agents received a letter from HR outlining all of the perks they received in their role—salary, benefits, vacation, etc. It was designed to remind the staff of how they personally benefitted from their jobs.

---

128 Adam M. Grant et al., "Impact and the art of motivation maintenance: The effects of contact with beneficiaries on persistent behavior," *Organizational Behavior and Human Decision Processes* 103, no. 1 (May 2007): 53-67, https://doi.org/10.1016/j.obhdp.2006.05.004.

Finally, in the task significance group, instead of highlighting how the agents' benefited in their role, each participant received a gratitude letter from one of the scholarship recipients. In it, the student explained how the funds were life-changing, creating an opportunity that would not have been possible without the efforts of the call center staff.

Since no one was allowed to speak about the experiment, agents in the task significance group could not tell callers about the heartfelt and moving thank you letter. Yet when professor Grant followed up with the three groups, the task significance group saw their weekly pledges increase from an average of nine pre-intervention to an average of twenty-three (an increase of almost 250 percent) post-intervention. What's more, the amount of donations received increased by an average of 171 percent.

In realizing the amazing impact of their work on the scholarship recipient, the task significance group reframed their work such that, rather than focusing on the fear of rejection, they thought about the potential opportunity that the next call represented—the chance to directly transform someone else's life.

4. Greater Motivation

When we feel that our work has meaning, that understanding directly impacts our motivation and, consequently, our productivity.

In a brilliant experiment conducted by behavioral economist Dan Ariely and colleagues, participants were asked to assemble Bionicles (humanoid figures consisting of modified Lego bricks and ball-and-socket joints) in exchange for a sliding scale of compensation, receiving $2 for the first figure, $1.89 for the second, and so on until they made twenty, at which point they were paid $.02 for each additional figure[129].

Participants were divided into two groups, "Meaningful" and "Sisyphus" (in reference to the Greek myth of a king sentenced to repeat a single task for all of eternity). When those in the Meaningful group turned in their figure, the researcher placed it on the desk and handed the participant a new box to assemble. In the Sisyphus group, however, there were only two boxes. As the participant completed a Bionicle, the researcher accepted it, handed the participant the other box to assemble, and then disassembled the completed figure immediately in full view.

Imagine yourself in this situation for a moment. Even though you are completely aware that this is an experiment, how would it impact your motivation to see your original figure taken apart and handed back to you to rebuild, over and over again?

Notably, this visible disassembly was the only difference between the two groups. In both cases, when participants completed a figure they were told how much they had earned and how much they would earn by making another one. At any point, they could decide to stop building and take their earnings.

Even though the participants knew that there was no greater meaning to building the figures other than their contribution to science, the Meaningful group showed significantly greater perseverance, constructing an average of 50 percent more figures compared to those individuals in the Sisyphus group.

"In our view," the researchers concluded, "meaning, at least in part, derives from the connection between work and some purpose, however insignificant or irrelevant that purpose may be to the worker's

---

129 Dan Ariely et al., "Mans Search for Meaning: The Case of Legos," *Journal of Economic Behavior & Organization* 67, no. 3-4 (2008): 671-77, doi:10.1016/j.jebo.2008.01.004.

personal goals. When that connection is severed, when there is no purpose, work becomes absurd, alienating, and even demeaning."

PRACTICING PURPOSEFUL LEADERSHIP

Practicing Purposeful Leadership

1. Find Greater Meaning in Your Work

2. "Outsource Inspiration"

3. Create a Shared Sense of Purpose

4. Identify Personal Core Values

5. Have More Meaningful Discussions With Your Employees

6. Spend Time Engaged in Meaningful Activities

In an effort to discover what influences work engagement and productivity, researchers Christine Porath and Tony Schwartz conducted a survey of more than 20,000 workers across a broad range of industries, with surprisingly consistent results. It turns out that we are happiest when four core needs are met: physical, emotional, mental, and spiritual, the latter being defined as "feeling connected to a higher purpose at work[130]."

In a separate study, Dr. Paul Fairlie pointed out that a 10 percent increase in *meaningful* work is linked to a 7 percent increase in satisfaction, commitment, intention to stay with the job, and lower burnout, as well as an almost 8 percent increase in engagement.

---

130 Tony Schwartz and Christine Porath, "Why You Hate Work," *The New York Times*, May 30, 2014, https://www.nytimes.com/2014/06/01/opinion/sunday/why-you-hate-work.html?_r=1.

With a sense of meaning and purpose being such a strong motivator, how can we encourage it more in the workplace?

1. Find Greater Meaning in Your Work

Traditionally, jobs are designed in a top-down fashion, with managers determining the needs of the company and then defining those roles accordingly. From there, applicants passively fill these roles without any opportunity to influence the original job description. Yet as the need for engendering purpose and meaning in work continues to rise, this approach has come under question and led to the notion of "job crafting."

Job crafting enables employees to alter their responsibilities in such a way that it creates greater meaning, resulting in positive effects on their performance, psychological well-being, and work engagement.

"Whether employees believe that their work contributes to making the world a better place, or that it allows them to interact with people in ways that create important innovations … work meanings [job crafting] act as lenses through which employees understand and respond to their work," Wrzesniewski states[131].

In observing two distinctly different job settings—a car manufacturing facility in Sweden and the role of special education professionals in a large public school district—Dr. Brenda Ghitulescu found that job crafting improved individual employees' job satisfaction and commitment and increased their performance. It also significantly reduced their rate of absenteeism. Ghitulescu concluded that the effects of job crafting appear to positively influence both individual and team outcomes.

---

131 For individuals who wish to learn more about job crafting, the Center for Positive Organizations has a wealth of information and resources.

Through job crafting, "workers can imbue their work with increased meaningfulness not necessarily through the kind of work they do, but more importantly through their relationship to their work and with others at work," Ghitulescu states[132].

Stepping back and reflecting on what is truly important in our roles, and how those qualities reflect our personal purpose, presents us with the opportunity to maximize our potential and benefit ourselves, our organizations, and the people we serve.

One simple way to begin this process with your team is by having them write down all of the tasks they engage in on a regular basis and determine the amount of time that is dedicated to each task. Then, have your employees rate the tasks on the degree to which they bring a deeper sense of meaning in their role. Armed with this information, you should have a clear idea of the extent to which employees currently experience meaning within their work, as well as opportunities for enhancing it. Then, you can set up a time to speak with your employees about this assessment and discuss ways in which you can bring more meaning into their roles.

CAN YOU DESCRIBE YOUR CALLING?

Drawing from Wrzeniewski and Dutton's work, Tal Ben-Shahar, a lecturer at Harvard, developed "calling descriptions." More than a job description, a calling description directs us to look at our role and responsibilities, and then challenges us to write them in a way that would encourage someone else to apply for our position. Par-

132 Brenda Elena Ghitulescu, "Shaping Tasks and Relationships At Work: Examining the Antecedents and Consequences of Employee Job Crafting," University of Pittsburgh, accessed December 6, 2018, http://d-scholarship.pitt.edu/10312/1/ghitulescube_etd.pdf.

ticipants have to consider the purpose of their activities, how they serve other people, and then how those things connect to their larger personal life goals.

For instance, consider how you would answer the following questions:

- Describe your job from the perspective of "selling" it to someone else. What would make an applicant excited to do what you do?

- What is the greater impact of your role?

- What impression do you personally and professionally hope to leave with others (clients and team members)?

- How could you craft your job title to more accurately describe who you are and what you do (ex: "Champion of Team Member Success" instead of "Human Resources Representative")?

Combined, the answers to these questions create a basic calling description. This practical spin on job crafting is an excellent means by which we can shift our perspective on the work we do and explore different elements that enhance its meaning.

2. "Outsource Inspiration"

"A growing body of research shows that end users ... are surprisingly effective in motivating people to work harder, smarter, and more productively," states Wharton professor Adam Grant[133]. In other words,

---

133 Adam Grant, "How Customers Can Rally Your Troops," *Harvard Business Review*, August 1, 2014, https://hbr.org/2011/06/how-customers-can-rally-your-troops.

"They [managers] *outsourced inspiration* to those who were better suited for the job."

By calling on customers to share how an organization's work directly affects their lives, leaders can provide team members with tangible proof that their efforts are having an important and lasting impact. Companies like Volvo, for instance, regularly tell their engineers stories of people who have survived horrific car crashes thanks to the design and integrity of the cars they produce. Medtronic routinely invites patients to their annual holiday parties so employees can hear firsthand how their medical technology prolonged, enriched, and/or saved lives. In each of these cases, the company is taking the time to step back and remind their employees, "This is *why* we exist."

3. Create a Shared Sense of Purpose

Daniel Pink, bestselling author of *Drive*, developed an exercise that I have often facilitated with my clients called, "Whose Purpose Is It, Anyway?" The idea is straightforward: members of a team are asked to individually write down the *purpose* of their company/division/team [Note that "purpose" here does not necessarily mean "moralistic." Employees could just as easily understand their company's purpose to "destroy our competition" as it could be to "end world hunger."]. Then the answers are shared within the group to determine the extent to which everyone is aligned. Regardless of the degree of similarity, sharing this information provides a wonderful opportunity for conversation.

If the answers vary significantly, this indicates that there is considerable value in having a collective conversation around the organization's core purpose. Alternately, if there is strong alignment among team members, yet that alignment is not in keeping with what the senior leadership wants to convey, then adjustments could be made to bring employee views in line. If everyone essentially agrees on their core purpose, this can be celebrated and leaders can ensure they continue doing what they have been doing.

In all cases, the critical question to answer is, "Does everyone have a shared understanding of why our organization exists?" If not, then steps need to be taken to make that purpose clear and universally understood, from encouraging team members to recite the company's core purpose during meetings for a small reward (such as a gift card) to posting it around the building and including it in inter-office communications.

4. Identify Personal Core Values

For Harry Kraemer, former CEO of Kellogg, living by our core values is crucial, especially for leaders. "Values-based leaders take the time to discover and reflect on what is most important to them," he writes in his book *From Values to Action: the Four Principles of Values-Based Leadership*. "Their objective is to make the world a better place within the scope of their influence, no matter how great or small."

Kraemer goes on to describe some of his core values as "… making a difference with my life—by treating others with respect and never focusing on my own needs or desires ahead of the goals of my team or organization."

Clearly defining our core values makes it much easier for us to honor and live them in our daily lives. Decision-making is simplified because in the end, if a certain course of action does not support a core value, or if it goes directly against one, then that option is clearly off the table.

Of course, there may be times when our core values seem to conflict with certain decisions. Choosing to spend more time at work, for instance, may conflict with a core value of "family always comes first." However, if we are working longer in order to spend more time with family on an upcoming vacation, or because the extra work pays for a child's education, then that time away from family is still, at its core, putting family first.

When we honor our core values, we feel that we are being true to ourselves. When we don't, we feel inauthentic, which is why knowledge of our core values is critical when it comes to our work environment. When values are misaligned, we have two options: either we find ways to bring our work and personal values closer together, or we start looking for another opportunity. Without that alignment, we will never feel "right" about our role.

How To Conduct a Values Audit

Many executives struggle with this alignment between personal and organizational core values. If, for instance, they are tasked with instituting a decision that the organization has made that does not fall in line with their values, then they are going to bear an extraordinary cost in upholding it because it does not feel good.

One powerful way to identify the extent to which our values overlap with those of our organization is to perform a Values Audit. The first step is to list five personal values that are most important to you. Then, on a scale of one to ten, rate how well *your employer* lives those values every day. At the same time, rate how well *your job* allows you to live each of your values every day. The information provided by these two scores helps you visualize the strength of your compatibility with the organization. In areas where there is a substantial disconnect, look for opportunities for improvement and determine the extent to which you can control that shift.

You can also ask each of your team members to conduct a Values Audit themselves. This accomplishes two important objectives.

First, it allows you to get to know each of your employees in a more meaningful way. This information can be valuable when it comes to task assignment, determining their priorities, etc. Second, it can also highlight potential values conflict and open the door for conversation. Can you fix the issue? Can you reframe it? Are there other ways to tackle it? Rather than having potentially damaging values conflict operating under the surface, a Values Audit brings them to the forefront and empowers you and your employees to address any possible concerns right away.

CLEARLY STATE YOUR ORGANIZATION'S VALUES

Organizational values should be clear to all employees from day one and leadership should regularly reinforce them. This can be done by:

- Leading by example and always making decisions based on the company's core values (and making that association clear, when possible. Ex: "Our organization gives employees $1,000/year for professional development because one of our core values is "Commitment to Lifelong Learning.")

- Informing everyone of company values, both through written communication and action.

- Reinforcing values whenever possible, working them into meetings, and other forms of inter-office communication.

- Rewarding and recognizing employees for knowing and living by the core values of the company.

NOT JUST A PAYCHECK

I routinely speak with executive coaching clients and audience members who share their personal stories about working in environments where their personal values did not align with those of their employer. Because of this, they opted to take jobs with less pay and which were lower in the hierarchy because those opportunities did what the higher paying ones could not—feed their souls[134].

This is a powerful statement regarding the importance of finding meaning in one's work. In investigating this question, Jing Hu and Jacob Hirsh discovered that on average, people are willing to take a 32 percent cut in pay if it meant that they could do more work, which they considered "generally meaningful, valuable, and worthwhile[135]."

Taking it a step further, Hu and Hirsh reviewed data from a work orientation survey administered to more than 43,000 participants, and determined that people were more likely to turn down a higher paying job at another organization if they found their present work to be more meaningful. This highlights why meaning matters and should be top of mind for any

---

134 Jing Hu and Jacob B. Hirsh, "Accepting Lower Salaries for Meaningful Work," *Frontiers*, September 7, 2017, https://www.frontiersin.org/articles/10.3389/fpsyg.2017.01649/full.

135 However, the researchers caution that there is no universally accepted definition of meaningful work. It is, indeed, a personal assessment: "... nearly half of the jobs that were described as 'meaningful' by at least one participant were also described as 'meaningless' by others, which indicates that meaning in work is highly subjective. Among the jobs ranked as meaningful or meaningless by participants were teacher, nurse, banker, writer, salesperson, and office worker."

executive who wishes to create highly engaged teams and organizations.

5. Have More Meaningful Discussions With Your Employees

We often hesitate to talk about the "touchy feely" side of work, yet these discussions are incredibly important. People want to know why and how their work matters.

How can we encourage more meaningful discussions? For one, leaders can talk about meaning and purpose more often in their day-to-day conversations, and make it a point to "walk the talk." Additionally, asking and/or telling employees how they are contributing to the overall purpose of the organization can lead to productive conversations. This discussion may also open the door for a deeper examination into how that person can contribute in a way that is even more meaningful to him or her.

> People want to know why and how their work matters.

Take a mortgage loan officer, for example. If her understanding of her company's core values includes "maximizing bank profits and squeezing clients for every last dollar," then she may not find a lot of meaning in her role (unless, of course, this aligns with one of her core values). If, however, her manager takes the time to explain that her job is "to support clients in achieving their life dream of owning a home and to help them do so without putting them at financial risk," then the deeper meaning of her role becomes clearer. She can look at her job as a way of supporting people, of guiding them on a financial path that is best for them. By doing so, those clients will likely have better financial success and consequently, refer others looking for similar results.

6. Spend Time Engaged in Meaningful Activities

It's unrealistic to believe that we can spend every waking hour of every day engaged in meaningful activities. This does not mean we cannot maximize the time we have available.

An excellent example of this practice comes from a study involving a population that has historically high levels of burnout: physicians. Researchers surveyed nearly five hundred doctors to explore the extent to which engaging in meaningful activities provided a significant buffer from stress.

For the vast majority of doctors in the study, their most meaningful activity was patient care. Despite its importance, however, most respondents noted they did not spend much of their time in this way, but rather were involved in lengthy paperwork and other non-patient-centric activities.

Interestingly, the less time doctors spent treating patients, the higher their burnout rate. For instance, doctors who spent less than 10 percent of their time engaged in patient care reported 57 percent burnout, while those who spent more than 20 percent of their time engaged in patient care reported half the level of burnout.

Meaningful work, then, appears to protect against stress and burnout. This is why I often advise my executive coaching clients to engage in a "Meaning Audit," as Laura did at the beginning of this chapter. This involves going through their calendar and determining how much of their time is spent in meaningful activities. Once the audit is completed, executives can see how much time they are engaging in these essential tasks and then adjust their schedule accordingly so they can do more of this type of work, while holding these appointments as sacred.

You can conduct your own Meaning Audit by first reflecting on what it is that truly excites you about your job (and if you can't think of anything, maybe it is time to consider a new role). Then look over your calendar for the past two weeks or so to see how much of your time was spent dedicated to these activities. If, like Laura, you spent little to no time engaged in these tasks, find time in your schedule to do it. Even a ten-minute window, once a day, is enough to remind you of why you do what you do. As you experience the profound benefits of this approach, look to where you can expand it, making the most meaningful part of what you do feature more prominently in your day-to-day work.

Once again, you can share this activity with your team to maximize their engagement and resilience.

THE PURPOSEFUL THOUGHT LEADER: SIMON SINEK

In his popular TED Talk "How Great Leaders Inspire Action," best-selling author Simon Sinek speaks to a concept he calls The Golden Circle. Most companies, he explains, talk about *what* they do. Some companies even talk about *how* they do it. However, very few companies talk about *why* they do it. This is an important distinction and one that separates the best leaders and the best organizations from the rest: the best start with why.

Take Sinek's example of Samuel Pierpont Langley and the Wright Brothers. While both had the same goal of powered man flight, Langley seemed the most likely to make it happen since he was funded by the War Department, held a seat at Harvard, and hired the brightest minds money could buy. The Wright brothers, on the other hand, had no money and no college education. Yet they were deeply driven by the meaning behind their pursuit because they believed that figuring out flight would fundamentally change the world, and the small team working with them believed the same thing.

Said a different way, although Langley simply knew *what* he wanted to achieve, the Wright brothers knew *why* they wanted to achieve it.

"If you hire people just because they can do a job, they'll work for your money," Sinek states. "But if you hire people who believe what you believe, they'll work for you with blood and sweat and tears."

This refocusing of perspective, from what to why, is at the heart of the Golden Circle. Drawn out, it describes three progressively smaller circles set within each other, much like a bullseye. The *what* of a company falls on the outermost circle as all companies know what they do. Apple, as Sinek explains, sells computers. That is their *what*.

The next smaller circle is *how* a company does what it does; that value or process that makes them unique. Most companies know their how, but not all, and many fail to see that their how is not the same as their purpose. In Sinek's example, how Apple is different is that it makes computers that are "beautifully designed, simple to use, and user friendly."

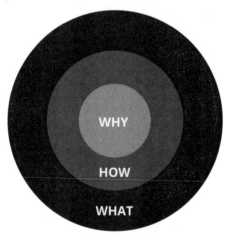

Source: Simon Sinek

The center of the Golden Circle is purpose; it is why a company does what it does. For Apple, their why is simply "In everything we do, we believe in challenging the status quo."

"Orville and Wilbur were driven by a cause, by a purpose, by a belief," Sinek says. "We follow those who lead, not because we have to, but because we want to. It's those who start with 'why' that have the ability to inspire those around them."

MEANING AND PURPOSE ON A CORPORATE SCALE: PROCTOR & GAMBLE

> "We follow those who lead, not because we have to, but because we want to. It's those who start with 'why' that have the ability to inspire those around them." —Simon Sinek

Stories have always played an important role in Robert McDonald's approach to leadership. The former CEO of Proctor & Gamble (P&G), McDonald began writing down his often-quoted anecdotes more than twenty years ago. Over time, as he reviewed and refined them, those stories evolved into his statement of beliefs.

"By writing down what you believe and sharing the results with the people you work with, everyone learns what's important to you," McDonald explained in an interview with his alma mater, Kennedy-Western University[136]. "I want a culture where every person in the organization is prepared to make a difference, and sharing what you believe, and why, helps create that kind of culture."

Before retiring from P&G in 2013, McDonald shared his "why" with colleagues, P&G managers, and others in a document titled "What I Believe In," a practice that he felt had a two-fold benefit:

1. It forced him to be much more deliberate about his leadership.

---

136 "Inside P&G's Digital Revolution," Kwu-alumni.org, November 2011, http://kwu-alumni.org/moto/media/55590ac35c5ee.pdf.

2. In knowing exactly what he believed in, people could call him out for not following through, consequently building stronger and more trusting relationships.

One important story that he notes early on in the document is the high value that P&G places on its core purpose of "touching and improving lives." In everything they did, McDonald wrote, P&G made sure that this purpose was evident. From the *Always* brand sponsoring education of menstruation to schoolgirls in Kenya, to *Pampers* leading a drive with UNICEF to vaccinate mothers against neonatal tetanus.

The Children's Safe Drinking Water program is another example of the organization's efforts to live its purpose. Since 2004, this program has brought more than 13 billion liters of clean water to those in need through an innovative water purification packet developed by P&G scientists, who discovered it while experimenting on ways to separate the dirt from dirty laundry water. With nothing more than a bucket, a stir stick, and a cloth, the packet can remove more than 99.9 percent of common waterborne bacteria, viruses, and protozoa in up to ten liters of water in thirty minutes[137]. This revelation led P&G to state that this program alone saves "one life every hour."

MCDONALD'S 10 CORE BELIEFS

1. Living a life driven by purpose is more meaningful and rewarding than meandering through life without direction.

---

137 "A Simple Way to Clean Water," P&G, https://csdw.org/pg-purifier-of-water-packets.

2. Companies must do well to do good and must do good to do well.

3. Everyone wants to succeed, and success is contagious.

4. Putting people in the right jobs is one of the most important jobs of the leader.

5. Character is the most important trait of a leader.

6. Diverse groups of people are more innovative than homogenous groups.

7. Ineffective systems and cultures are bigger barriers to achievement than the talents of people.

8. There will be some people in the organization who will not make it on the journey.

9. Organizations must renew themselves.

10. The true test of the leader is the performance of the organization when they are absent or after they depart.

"You can't say you are about making life better for people only in one area of your business," McDonald writes. "It has to be meaningfully integrated into all aspects of your business and operations."

PILLAR 6

EMPATHY

Seek first to understand, then to be understood.

—Stephen Covey

When I started working with Nathaniel, he was concerned that his natural tendencies were interfering with his leadership potential. He was incredibly intellectual, yet he understood both through his own awareness as well as from external feedback that his approach was not going over well with co-workers. So he asked me to conduct a psychometric assessment in order to provide evidence-based insight into the issue.

When his results came back, he was not at all surprised to learn that he had an extraordinarily high IQ. He was also not taken aback when we found that he scored in the absolute lowest percentile for empathy. In fact, he joked that his style was best suited for a dictatorship.

Unfortunately, his intellectual gifts and technical know-how led Nathaniel to engage in the frustrating habit of zeroing in on the "right" answer when speaking with his colleagues, employees, or clients. He routinely bowled over others' suggestions, leaving a trail of bruised egos in his wake; so much so that, in time, people eventually stopped contributing during meetings because they felt their opinions did not matter or that they would be lambasted for their stupidity.

While he found dark humor in the fact that he was "built to be a dictator," he readily understood that his lack of empathy was a major stumbling block for his career. Yet he did not believe there was anything he could do about it.

"Is it even possible to learn empathy?" he asked me. And my reply was the first thing that day to surprise him.

"Yes," I said. "It is absolutely possible."

EMPATHY CAN BE LEARNED

On observing the profound impact of empathy as it relates to improved patient satisfaction, better patient adherence to treatment protocols, and increased well-being in doctors, Dr. Helen Riess, an Associate Clinical Professor of Psychiatry at Harvard Medical School and Director of the Empathy and Relational Science Program at Massachusetts General Hospital, set out to explore whether it was possible to bring about observable improvements in physician empathy.

Drawing on Daniel Goleman's work in the area of emotional intelligence, as well as elements of the neuroscience of empathy, Dr. Reiss designed and implemented an empathy training program for physicians[138]. Tests of the program revealed increased levels of empathy in doctors as reported by their patients, and the doctors also felt the content was immensely valuable and relevant to their work.

One powerful aspect of the program involved measuring the physiological reactions of patients to physicians' positive or negative displays of empathy through watching videos of their interactions. As Dr. Riess explained to me, "Our learners could see the actual physical impacts of rude and dismissive behaviors on other people. As one person put it, 'It feels like I am looking at an x-ray of a person's psyche.'"

Using Dr. Riess' groundbreaking empathy research as a foundation, Nathaniel and I looked at concrete ways in which he could exhibit empathy, starting with everyday conversations. Instead of constantly talking about work, I encouraged Nathaniel to be more curious about other people—what they did outside of work and what excited them about their role in the organization. Rather than talking over or correcting them, he would exercise more patience and ensure that others finished their thoughts. His increased focus on questioning would facilitate this. His overarching goal was to become a conversational Sherlock Holmes, gathering as many clues about that individual as possible. He would also keep detailed notes of each person so he could reference them in future conversations.

As a result of his efforts, Nathaniel's subsequent 360 feedback scores increased not just in regard to empathy, but across the board. The fact that he began talking with and demonstrating interest in his fellow team members paid tremendous dividends to his overall leadership effectiveness.

---

138 Daniel Goleman and Richard E. Boyatzis, "Emotional Intelligence Has 12 Elements. Which Do You Need to Work On?" *Harvard Business Review*, December 5, 2017, https://hbr.org/2017/02/emotional-intelligence-has-12-elements-which-do-you-need-to-work-on.

I'll never forget what he said to me after we reviewed his improved scores:

"I'm probably never going to be the guy who's naturally interested in people," Nathaniel said. "At the same time, I completely understand the benefits of asking people questions and getting to know them. It's fascinating how it gets others to talk to you and open up."

It was an amazing evolution to observe. For someone who was initially skeptical, putting a few techniques into practice allowed him to discover and directly experience the value of empathy.

DEFINING EMPATHY

Empathy is being aware of the thoughts, feelings, and experiences of others without necessarily walking in their shoes. In 1996, nursing scholar Theresa Wiseman published "A Concept Analysis of Empathy" in which she divided empathy into four defining attributes[139]:

1. See the world as others see it: recognize that their reality is their truth.

2. Practice non-judgment: accept people for who they are.

3. Understand another's feelings: realize what they're experiencing on an emotional level.

4. Communicate that understanding: share in such a way that they know we understand where they're coming from.

For instance, imagine a leader has an employee who suddenly starts causing issues with other team members. He is lashing out, snapping at co-workers, and is generally difficult to work with. Knowing that this person is normally not like this, the leader sets

---

139 Theresa Wiseman, "A concept analysis of empathy," *Journal of Advanced Nursing* 23 (1996): 1162-1167, 10.1046/j.1365-2648.1996.12213.x.

up a meeting to discuss what is going on. In the course of the conversation, the employee reveals that he has been diagnosed with skin cancer and while it is still at stage one, he is frightened about what may happen next.

By leading with empathy, the leader can see how these angry episodes are a logical manifestation of the employee's anxiety. His world suddenly appears to have a very immediate endpoint and he is terrified. In accepting this without judgment and by expressing understanding that anger is a natural stage of grief, the leader handles the discussion with empathy, and the employee walks away feeling as though he has been heard. Consequently, the employee also understands how he has been acting and, with the knowledge that his leader understands what he is going though, he is able to better control his outbursts.

This is a model case because it contains all of the attributes of empathy: the leader listens to what the employee has to say, sees it from his point of view, does not judge him for his reaction, and communicates that understanding to him.

EMPATHY IS BECOMING THE MOST DESIRED SOFT SKILL IN BUSINESS

Over the past forty-plus years, there has been a significant shift toward the importance of empathy. In 1970, the top three skills required to work in a Fortune 500 company were reading, writing, and arithmetic. In 1999, those skills had evolved into problem solving, interpersonal skills, and teamwork[140].

---

140 Melissa Jun Rowley, "Why It's Time to Rethink the Role of Business in Education," *The Huffington Post*, December 7, 2017, https://www.huffingtonpost.com/melissa-jun-rowley/why-its-time-to-rethink-t_1_b_4878092.html.

According to LinkedIn, empathy is the number one job skill to have in 2020[141]. Heavy-hitting companies are already incorporating empathy into their hiring criteria. Lazlo Bock of Google famously stated to *The New York Times*, "GPAs are worthless as a criteria for hiring ... We found that they don't predict anything[142]."

THE SCIENCE OF EMPATHETIC LEADERSHIP

The Science of Empathetic Leadership

1. Superior Performance

2. Effective Leadership

3. Better Bottom Line

As the saying goes, "No one cares how much you know until they know how much you care[143]." The following highlights the benefits of exhibiting empathy based on the existing research:

1. Superior Performance

Why does empathy matter? Consider the study conducted by Yehonatan Turner, radiology resident at Shaare Zedek Medical Center in Jerusalem, Israel, in which he and his colleagues examined

---

141 George Anders, "The Number One Job Skill in 2020," LinkedIn, June 11, 2013, https://www.linkedin.com/ pulse/20130611180041-59549-the-no-1-job-skill-in-2020/.

142 Adam Bryant, "In Head-Hunting, Big Data May Not Be Such a Big Deal," *The New York Times*, June 20, 2013, http://www.nytimes.com/2013/06/20/business/in-head-hunting-big-data-may-not-be-such-a-big-deal.html.

143 While this saying has often been attributed to former US president Theodore Roosevelt, its source remains unverified.

whether or not the limited contact that x-ray technicians have with patients played a part in their diagnosis[144]. Specifically, the researchers were curious as to whether including photos of the patients along with their medical image would alter the results.

Every single one of the radiologists in the study reported feeling more empathy toward the patients when pictures were included and, in fact, learned more about the patient from the photos, such as recognizing physical signs of disease or suffering. Their reports were also 29 percent longer on average than those without pictures, and their diagnostic accuracy jumped by a whopping 46 percent.

Additionally, the rate of incidental findings—those abnormalities spotted by radiologists that were not a part of the original exam—increased by 80 percent.

Without the pictures, the medical images became remote, dehumanized; they were simply data points. Yet when the radiologists saw exactly who would be impacted by their analysis, an empathetic connection was triggered and their diagnoses improved.

THE PHYSICIAN-BUSINESS LEADER PARALLEL

Another impressive study outlining the benefits of empathy involved more than 21,000 diabetic patients and over two hundred doctors[145].

Doctors were initially rated by their patients as being low, moderate, or high in empathy. Then the patients were asked about any diabetic complica-

---

144 Radiological Society of North America, "Patient Photos Spur Radiologist Empathy And Eye For Detail," ScienceDaily, accessed May 17, 2018, www.sciencedaily.com/releases/2008/12/081202080809.htm.

145 Stefano Del Canale et al., "The Relationship Between Physician Empathy and Disease Complications," *Academic Medicine* 87, no. 9 (2012): 1243-249, doi:10.1097/acm.0b013e3182628fbf.

tions they had experienced. In analyzing the data, the researchers discovered that not only did patients with high-empathy doctors experience significantly fewer complications, these patients were also more likely to comply with their treatment regimens. Additionally, patients with high-empathy doctors were more likely to report symptoms or concerns, thus enabling the physicians to provide higher quality care.

This makes intuitive sense. When we feel understood, we're much more inclined to open up and talk about things that are often uncomfortable to discuss.

What's more, patients with high-empathy doctors reported significantly greater satisfaction with their quality of care, and those doctors also had markedly fewer malpractice claims.

There are many powerful parallels between leadership and medical doctors. If we look at team members as "patients," for instance, a highly empathetic leader is more likely to have a compliant team since team members trust that the leader is making decisions in their best interest. Team members are also more likely to report "symptoms" as they arise, such as barriers to completing a certain project, allowing the leader to be more proactive in implementing solutions.

2. Effective Leadership

The Management Research Group (MRG) has administered its 360-degree feedback tool, the Leadership Effectiveness Analysis (LEA), to executives for more than thirty years[146]. In one of its landmark studies based on data collected from more than half a million leaders, MRG examined which of their twenty-two competencies were the most strongly linked to leadership excellence. Empathy, it turned out, was the third-strongest predictor. Number two was communication and the top predictor was strategic thinking.

To me, what's really interesting is not just the fact that empathy is such a strong predictor of executive excellence—we can also make a compelling argument as to how empathy informs both our ability to think strategically as well as our ability to communicate. In terms of the former, how can we create a compelling and effective strategy if we are neither aware of nor considering the impacts of our actions and decisions on the stakeholders we serve? In terms of the latter, how can we communicate effectively if we don't understand the needs of our audience?

EMPATHY IN LETTING PEOPLE GO

In discussing the importance of empathy when it comes to effective and strong leadership, a CEO shared a compelling example of how it played a valuable role in a very difficult decision.

While his organization owed much of its success to the creation and expansion of one of its larger divisions, shifts in technology and globalization had limited its shelf-life. Although countless efforts had been made to optimize and repurpose this area, the data was overwhelming.

---

146 See the appendix for a full list of the LEA's twenty-two behavioral leadership practices and six core leadership functions.

"We had to make an excruciating decision for the good of the overall business," he said. "And that was to let go of all of these amazing people who had supported us over the years and close the division down."

Once the reality of this decision had sunk in, the next question was, "How are we going to do this?"

Above all, the CEO wanted to make sure it was done empathetically. Despite strong opposition from some members of his senior executive team, the CEO decided to explain to the group exactly what was going on right away and why they needed to close the division. Once he delivered the difficult news, he also told the affected employees that he and the executive team would be collaborating with them to determine the best way to handle this decision.

Even though there was expressed concern that this early heads up would give the affected employees time to retaliate by sabotaging the company or exiting early, the CEO argued that it was worth the risk.

Despite his belief that it was the right thing to do, the CEO admitted that he was impressed and pleas-antly surprised by how engaged divisional employees were in making sure their part of the business was shut down correctly. While they were disappointed by the decision, there was no sabotage, nothing was destroyed, and even though a few people left early, the vast majority stayed and worked diligently until the end, with some even working overtime on the last day to ensure everything was done properly.

This is a powerful example for leaders who may believe that empathy prohibits them from making tough business decisions. We can still make tough decisions; it is how we implement them that matters.

3. Better Bottom Line

The Global Empathy Index, as developed by Belinda Parmar and her colleagues, asks "Which companies are successfully creating empathetic cultures?"

To answer this question, Parmar and her team analyze five categories they have identified as comprising empathy: ethics, company culture, brand perception, public messaging through social media, and leadership. Metrics to gauge these categories are then pulled from publicly available data such as the S&P Capital IQ, Glassdoor employee information, and accounting infractions and scandals.

In 2015, the Global Empathy Index showed that the top ten most empathetic companies also generated 50 percent more earnings than, and boasted twice the value of, the bottom ten[147].

One example of the resounding impact empathy can have on the bottom line is the case of Ryanair, which Parmar described in an

---

147 Top Ten Most Empathetic Companies of 2015 According to the Global Empathy Index:
1) LinkedIn (technology)
2) Microsoft (technology)
3) Audi (automotive)
4) Three (telecommunications)
5) John Lewis Partnership (retail)
6) Sony (technology)
7) Google (technology)
8) Nike (sports and retail)
9) Direct Line (insurance)
10) Boots UK (retail)

article for the *Harvard Business Review*[148]. In 2014, the Irish airline launched its "Always Getting Better" program, which looked specifically at pain points their customers were experiencing—such as the hassles associated with regular business travel or traveling with family—and created new services to relieve those issues[149].

On observing the company's net profit increase following the launch of the Always Getting Better program (rising from €867 million in 2015 to €1.24 billion in the year ending March 2016), Ryanair CEO Michael O'Leary famously stated, "If I'd only known being nice to customers was going to work so well, I'd have started many years ago[150]."

PRACTICING EMPATHETIC LEADERSHIP

Practicing Empathetic Leadership

1. Stop Focusing on Yourself

2. Visit the Front Lines

3. AMPPlify Your Listening

4. Break the Golden Rule

5. Incorporate "Capacity for Empathy" into Hiring and Promotions

---

148 Belinda Parmar, "The Most Empathetic Companies, 2016," *Harvard Business Review*, March 26, 2018, https://hbr.org/2016/12/the-most-and-least-empathetic-companies-2016.

149 Official Ryanair Website | Ryanair.com, https://www.ryanair.com/gb/en/useful-info/about-ryanair/always-getting-better.

150 Kari Lundgren, "Ryanair's O'Leary: Who Knew Being Nice Could Be So Profitable?" Bloomberg, May 26, 2015, https://www.bloomberg.com/news/articles/2015-05-26/ryanair-s-o-leary-who-knew-being-nice-could-be-so-profitable-.

Empathy has proven time and again to be an incredible asset in business. Equally, if not more importantly, it is not just a fixed ability, but a skill that can be learned and developed, as we learned from Nathaniel—the self-described dictator at the beginning of this chapter. Given the above findings, how can we become more empathetic leaders?

1. Stop Focusing on Yourself

People sometimes see what they want and drive their agenda forward without considering the desires or needs of others, or how they can help.

A recurring theme in many of my CEO interviews is that one of the biggest derailers of success is founders having an unyielding belief that their ideas are foolproof, despite feedback to the contrary. They believe that everyone wants what they have to offer. They do not ask how it should be packaged or marketed; they simply believe that because they think it's a great idea, then everyone else will, as well.

The marketing history of Febreze is an excellent example of how this phenomenon almost upended an incredible success story. Despite having a product that eliminated household odors, its sales were very disappointing. So the company decided to conduct a series of focus groups to figure out why.

Their research revealed that while consumers felt that the product worked extremely well, it did not leave them feeling things smelled "clean." So the company went back to the drawing board and came up with the Febreze we recognize today, which features a variety of scents that leave a room smelling "clean," even though the smell itself has no cleaning value whatsoever.

The developers of Febreze had a brilliant idea, but in not considering how others would perceive their product, they almost missed out on an opportunity to be a frontrunner in what would eventually become a billion dollar industry.

2. Visit the Front Lines

A compelling example of the power of visiting the front line is seen in the show *Undercover Boss*. In one episode, the CEO of Philly Pretzel Company, Dan DiZio, posed as an entry-level worker in some of the chain's one hundred twenty locations on the east coast[151]. During one of his stops, he got to know Bill, a franchise owner who could barely afford his location and had introduced a pepperoni pretzel roll that was well accepted by the community yet was not approved by the corporate office. He had reached out several times for approval, but with no response. At another location, DiZio met a young man, Marques, who worked sixty hours a week to support his family, yet was looking for a new job because he needed benefits.

"I thought that, because I was a founder of the company, and that I had twisted pretzels, that I would never forget all that," said DiZio in an interview with AOL Jobs. "You don't want to become that CEO that's out of touch. But I lost perspective."

As a result of his experiences, DiZio stated that he would make it a point to visit all one hundred twenty of his locations every year, and would continue to actively learn from his staff's frontline experiences.

"The person who has been on the floor will have the answers," DiZio said. "Every CEO needs to go undercover in their company."

151 Dan Fastenberg, "'Undercover Boss': Pretzel CEO In A Twist Over Working Conditions," AOL, July 15, 2016, https://www.aol.com/2012/04/28/undercover-boss-pretzel-ceo-in-a-twist-over-working-conditio/.

3. AMPPlify Your Listening

In their book *Crucial Conversations*, authors Kerry Patterson, Joseph Grenny, Al Switzler, and Ron McMillan argue that, "The root cause of many—if not most—human problems lies in how people behave when others disagree with them about high stakes, emotional issues." Based on this reality, the authors suggest several ways in which we can engage in constructive conversations during these highly emotional times. One approach they present is the AMPP model for power listening, which stands for:

A: Ask

The first step, asking, gets things rolling. As we learned from Dr. Marilee Adams in the chapter on civility, being aware of our mind-set when interacting with others helps us ask more powerful questions. When we are in learning mode, for instance, we are more open, flexible, and connected to the conversation. By showing a genuine interest in what's going on with the other person, we are able to bring potential issues to light. What better avenue do we have to learn another person's reality than to ask them?

In 2004, researchers Marcial Losada and Emily Heaphy showed that the highest performing teams spent more time asking questions compared to their lower performing counterparts[152]. The top teams had an inquiry to advocacy ratio of 1:1, wherein every time an executive advocated their position, they also asked a question. In the lowest-performing teams, the ratio was closer to 1:20, with questions being asked once out of every twenty statements.

152 M. Losada and E.D. Heaphy, "The Role of Positivity and Connectivity in the Performance of Business Teams: A Nonlinear Dynamics Model," *American Behavioral Scientist* 47, (2004): 740-756, DOI: 10.1177/0002764203260208.

When we think about meetings with very few questions, there is likely little changing of perspective taking place. Instead, participants are listening only to hear when the other person stops talking so they could state their (often contrarian) opinion.

On the other hand, asking questions—ideally those that are genuinely motivated by a desire to learn and discover new possibilities—invites others to participate and contribute their ideas. Ultimately, asking positive questions breaks down boundaries and fosters innovation.

M: Mirror

In order to engage in the difficult, yet necessary, conversations that are inherent to leadership roles, one of the areas that leaders must learn to master is conflict management and mirroring can be an excellent first step in the process.

Suppose you're sitting across from someone having a conversation, when suddenly the other person leans back, arms folded. No words are exchanged, yet we sense something is wrong. If asked, "How are you doing?" The reply is often a highly non-committal "Fine, fine."

In this case, mirroring becomes a powerful tool to explore what we just noticed, providing the other person with a mirror of the situation:

"Although I hear you say you're fine, based on your body language and tone of voice, I'm picking up that maybe you are not. I recognize I may be wrong. I wanted to check in because your engagement is very important to me."

We communicate far more with our nonverbals than we do with our words. In fact, psychologist and researcher Albert Mehrabian was the first to suggest the minimal value of words, indicating that the meaning we assign to communication consists of 55 percent body language, 38 percent tone of voice, and 7 percent the actual words spoken[153].

Barbara and Allan Pease, authors of *The Definitive Book of Body Language*, upheld the greater value of nonverbal cues in their analysis of thousands of recorded sales interviews, which "... showed that, in business encounters, body language accounts for between 60 and 80 percent of the impact made around a negotiating table." They added that, "Overall, we make our final decisions more on what we see than what we hear[154]."

Barb Stegmann, CEO of 7 Virtues, put it best when she said to me, "Everyone can learn to read body language. I think it is one of the key ingredients to strong leadership."

P: Paraphrase

Whether we get it right or wrong, paraphrasing is an excellent way to demonstrate empathy and to show that we are actively listening. When we get it right, the other person is satisfied that we understood what was said. When we are wrong, it gives the other person the opportunity to correct us; an action that many of us, deep down, actually enjoy.

A colleague of mine brilliantly capitalized on this technique to draw out more quiet individuals. During a conversation in which she felt she did not have the whole picture, she would intentionally mis-paraphrase the other person. This caused the individual to correct

---

153 Jeff Thompson, "Is Nonverbal Communication a Numbers Game?" Psychology Today, September 30, 2011, https://www.psychologytoday.com/us/blog/beyond-words/201109/is-nonverbal-communication-numbers-game.

154 Allan Pease and Barbara Pease, "'The Definitive Book of Body Language,'" *The New York Times*, September 24, 2006, https://www.nytimes.com/2006/09/24/books/chapters/0924-1st-peas.html.

her, which led to greater understanding and, more often than not, even more information.

Whether our paraphrasing is accurate is almost irrelevant. What really matters is the fact that we are making the effort to understand the other person.

P: Prime

Lastly, "prime" means that if there is an elephant in the room, we need to declare it. If we do not, people will likely think one of two things: either we do not care about the issue, or we are not smart enough to recognize that there is one.

Each of these options is undesirable, so we might as well name the elephant from the outset. For instance, when entering into a conflict management situation with two upset employees, a leader could prime the conversation with an opening statement such as:

"I appreciate that this may be a challenging conversation for all of us. My goal is to have a constructive dialogue; to be as positive and forward-looking as possible so that we can understand each other's perspectives and come to a win-win that we each feel good about. Although it may not be perfect, and there may be some contentious disagreements, I feel this is the right thing to do and I'm counting on the fact that we can do this together. What do you say?"

This script also works if we are in conflict with one (or more) individual(s).

Remember, by priming the conversation, we are ultimately seeking the other party's cooperation to come up with a solution that respects everyone's needs.

4. Break the Golden Rule

The "Golden Rule" ethic of "Treat others the way you wish to be treated" is a central organizing life principle for the vast majority of people worldwide. However, at its core, the Golden Rule is deeply flawed. When I share this observation with audiences, they are often shocked to hear it. Some raise their hands and challenge me, especially when they have learned this edict from one or both of their parents.

As we explore the tenet of the rule, I ask people to think about what could be wrong with it. They quickly realize that it does not encourage you to think about what the other person wants. Instead, it asks you to think about what *you* would want in the same situation and do the same for someone else.

No one has potentially exemplified this better than an audience member who came up to me after a keynote to share his story.

"I'm so glad you talked about this today," he said. "I've been happily married to my wife for thirty-five years and every year on my birthday, she makes me chocolate cake, and I never knew why. I hate chocolate cake. But it's her favorite kind of cake, so now it totally makes sense!"

To demonstrate empathy, we cannot live by the Golden Rule. Instead, we must live by the Platinum Rule: treat others the way *they* want to be treated.

In his bestseller *Give and Take*, Adam Grant gives the example of gifts brought by wedding guests. When gift registries are provided, more often than not, the guests who feel they "know" the couple best tend to ignore this guidance and instead purchase a "more meaningful" gift—something that represents the breadth and depth of their "special" relationship.

In following up with these couples, however, these "unique" gifts are rated much lower in terms of satisfaction and meaning than the gifts purchased from the registry, which suggests that they fall short on the very thing they are designed to do (e.g. be seen as more special).

The perils of following the Golden Rule are also evident when it comes to leadership. Research conducted by Hogan Assessments has demonstrated that managers tend to reward and recognize team members based on how the managers themselves would like to be rewarded and recognized. For example, if a manager loves to be brought up on stage and publicly acknowledged for an achievement, then he or she is likely to assume others will value the same kind of recognition.

To make sure any recognition has the desired impact, managers should first ask each of their team members how they like to be recognized to counteract any potential empathy gap.

5. Incorporate "Capacity for Empathy" into Hiring and Promotions

Organizations often look at technical expertise or intellectual horsepower when it comes to hiring. Yet, as we learned from Google's Lazlo Bock earlier in this chapter, GPAs and test scores offer very little predictive value in terms of how well someone will perform in their role.

As a hiring practice, empathy can be gauged through a psychometric assessment, such as the EQ-i or the Hogan EQ, or through empathy-related questions integrated into a structured interview process. For instance, candidates can be encouraged to talk about challenges at past jobs wherein they exhibited empathy.

When it comes to promotions, consider what behaviors you are rewarding. If the only people getting ahead are those who push others down or ruthlessly look out for and promote their own interests, then this standard will likely drive out high empathy individuals from your organization. If you truly value empathy, it needs to be recognized. Otherwise, there is no way for employees to see the importance of demonstrating it.

LIKE OIL AND WATER, EMPATHY AND EMAIL DO NOT MIX

With body language and tone of voice absent, the dismal 7 percent of meaning assigned to words that occurs in face-to-face interactions suddenly becomes 100 percent when the same message is conveyed via text or email. This presents a tremendous challenge, as we have no method of accessing the crucial remaining 93 percent of communication. We may believe a message we are sending reads positively, yet when it is received, that person may read it in an entirely different tone; likely one that is far more negative than we intended.

Emoticons, or emojis, are one attempt at getting around this electronic communication challenge, yet even those are often misinterpreted. Instead of taking a smile at face value, a recipient may interpret it as sarcastic or even condescending.

If a message is so important that you feel the need to write the perfect email, think again. Pick up the phone or, better yet, speak to the person face-to-face. There is far too great a risk of miscommunication when you can only convey a small part of the meaning behind the message.

THE EMPATHETIC CEO: NEIL BLUMENTHAL

It may be with a little tongue-in-cheek that Warby Parker CEO Neil Blumenthal declares how important it is to "see things from the other person's perspective[155]."

In describing the work he does through the vision company's nonprofit, VisionSpring, Blumenthal shared a particular moment in which empathy played a powerful role.

"I was in a village in rural Bangladesh, talking to a community of weavers. I knew they had vision problems, but no one was wearing glasses. I would say, 'Raise your hand if you have trouble seeing,' yet no one would raise their hands.

"So I said, 'Raise your hand if you have trouble threading a needle.' Then, everyone raised their hands."

In switching perspectives and putting himself in the weavers' place, Blumenthal figured out how to ask the question that he needed answered—a practice in empathy that he uses regularly at work.

Warby Parker applies these same principles in their approach to talent management. They make it a point to learn as much as they can about each of their employees and find out what gets them out of bed in the morning. With an understanding of their motivation in mind, the organization is much more capable of helping their employees find the path that fits them best—a practice they encourage in all of their company leaders.

---

155 Leigh Buchanan, "Warby Parker CEO: Why Empathy Matters," *Inc.*, May 29, 2013, https://www.inc.com/magazine/201306/leigh-buchanan/neil-blumenthal-warby-parker-why-empathy-matters.html.

EMPATHY ON A CORPORATE SCALE: ADOBE

When employees are empathetic toward the customer experience, the quality of that experience is far more likely to improve. This conclusion is what led computer software giant Adobe to combine the management of its employee and customer experience into one focus area.

"The two ideas go hand in hand," writes *Forbes* contributor Blake Morgan[156]. "Satisfied and engaged employees are more likely to give their best effort and represent the brand well, while satisfied customers are happier and easier to work with."

However, to bring these two areas together, Adobe had to change its mind-set: instead of employee/customer, the focus became "people" and how the role of one played into the experience of the other. For instance, Adobe encourages all employees to basically become customers, using the same products and reporting issues quickly. Compensation is also incentivized by customer satisfaction, and managers regularly check in with employees to gauge how connected employees feel with their customers; a connection that is greatly facilitated by the company's focus on empathy.

"Instead of simply getting a customer to make a sale or pushing an employee to hit their quarterly goals, organizations should look for ways to build lasting relationships that keep customers satisfied and coming back for more," states Morgan. "An often overlooked aspect of building [those] relationships is focusing on empathy and understanding where people come from."

In fact, "customer empathy" is listed as one of four key characteristics Adobe looks for in new hires, stating "We're looking for

---

156 Blake Morgan, "Leading Both Employee And Customer Experience At Adobe," *Forbes*, September 26, 2017, https://www.forbes.com/sites/blakemorgan/2017/09/26/leading-both-employee-and-customer-experience-at-adobe/#67ae49343c39.

employees who have OCD—obsessive customer DNA. They are individuals who lead first with customer needs and always innovative on behalf of what's best for the customer[157]."

---

157 "Adobe Systems Incorporated," Great Place to Work Reviews, accessed August 21, 2018, http://reviews.greatplacetowork.com/adobe-systems-incorporated.

CHALLENGE THE STATUS QUO

Poor leadership is not necessarily a reflection of the person. Plenty of good people are, and can be, poor leaders. The good news is that positive leadership is a skill; it can be learned, regardless of age, position, or experience. You can challenge the status quo of zero sum leadership by becoming a more positive leader—a powerful skill gained by practicing each of the core pillars discussed in this book.

When it comes to self-awareness, constantly seek out specific and candid feedback from your team, your colleagues, your supervisors, and your clients and stakeholders about how you are doing and how you can continue to improve.

By asking the people around you for their feedback, you are also showing respect, as you are letting them know that you value their opinions and that you are serious about improving, both as a leader and as a person. Also make sure to thank people when they support you in your efforts. This is another hallmark of respect.

Feedback conversations also showcase your humility. By seeking input and advice, you recognize that you do not have all of the answers; that you need the help of your community to better yourself.

Effectively mastering these skills also requires focusing on the positive. Adopting and/or expanding leadership practices is a marathon, not a sprint. Although setbacks will occur, they are a part of the process. Remember the acronyms for F.A.I.L. = From Action I Learn and First Attempt in Learning. While you do not want to ignore your missteps, do not focus all of your time and energy there. Remember to celebrate your wins, no matter how small. Acknowledge and recognize the progress you have made. Keep a positive attitude. These practices are essential to becoming a positive leader.

You also can foster a sense of meaning and purpose by discovering why positive leadership matters to you. What purpose does it serve? How does it benefit you and the people around you? Being clear on why you want to be a positive leader maximizes the chances you will get there. Once you have found your leadership why, share it with the people closest to you. This clearly shows them why these changes matter to you, which will inspire them to be more actively involved in, and supportive of, your efforts.

Empathy, the ability to take the perspective of others, is another excellent skill gained in the journey toward positive leadership. Thinking about the world through the eyes of your employees and stakeholders better equips you to deal with their concerns. Asking questions of your environment provides you invaluable insight that will serve you in every domain of your personal and professional life.

A WORD OF WARNING

As with learning any new skill, these pillars may feel foreign and perhaps even awkward, especially at the beginning. Understand that developing a new leadership practice takes time and commitment. That's okay. It is important to be kind to yourself as you make mistakes. The key is to learn from these experiences and keep pressing forward, being honest with yourself and others about how you are doing.

Clients I have worked with are often surprised at how good it feels to put these pillars into practice, and how effective they are at improving their relationships and performance. Their teams trust and respect them more as a result of their openness and commitment to improving their leadership approach. Although changing one's behavior can be challenging at first, the excitement my clients express when they are able to successfully apply these principles is extraordinary.

There are many ways to implement these pillars in your daily life. It is important that you find the techniques that work best for you and your situation. Partnering with a skilled coach can be incredibly beneficial, as he or she can help guide and support you through your leadership development, and help you figure out the best approach for you.

The following pages are designed to help you track your leadership goals using each of the Six Pillars. Each page identifies one of the pillars and provides a space in which to write down three goals for each pillar. You can then identify the actions you can take immediately, as well as in the short- and long-term to achieve these goals. Refer back to them often and use them to discuss your leadership development with your boss, your team, your coach, and anyone else who can hold you accountable.

WHY IS WRITING DOWN YOUR GOALS IMPORTANT?

Dr. Gail Matthews, a professor of psychology at the Dominican University in California, conducted research looking into the art and science of goal setting. She recruited a diverse group of 267 men and women from all over the world to participate in her study. These individuals came from all walks of life, including entrepreneurs, healthcare professionals, artists, lawyers, and bankers.

She divided the participants into groups, according to whether they wrote down their goals. Her results were fascinating and showcased the power of the written word. People who wrote down their goals achieved them at a significantly higher level than those who did not. In fact, your chances of goal attainment increase by **42 percent, simply by writing down your goals on a regular basis**.

Another powerful finding from Dr. Matthews' research was that the chances of goal attainment were also significantly increased when the participants shared their written goals with an accountability partner; someone who kept them focused and on track.

To honor this second finding, I will be forming a LinkedIn group for positive leaders who purchase this book where you can share your goals with other supportive and interested parties. Please reach out to me (craig@craigdowden.com) and join this network. Together we can achieve extraordinary results and build positive leaders around the world.

I hope that the stories, studies, and insights shared in this book have spoken to you, and that you have a greater understanding of what it takes to be a positive leader. Leadership is an ongoing process, so I do hope that you return to these pages for guidance or inspiration throughout your journey. Know that you do not take this road alone—there are many leaders who are seeking to improve. I welcome the opportunity to hear from you about your personal leadership journey. I also encourage you to reach out to the leaders around you so you can support each other. Better yet, join our LinkedIn community of positive leaders.

At its very core, positive leadership is about living the example, and knowing that in doing good, you will always lead well.

PILLAR 1: SELF-AWARENESS

I think self-awareness is probably the most important thing towards being a champion.

—Billie Jean King

Definition of Self-Awareness:

Self-awareness is having an accurate sense of who you are and how other people perceive you.

Why Self-Awareness Matters:

1. Improved Financial Performance

2. Higher Levels of Personal and Professional Success

3. Greater Job Fit and Organizational Success

Putting Self-Awareness Into Action:

1. Conduct a Personality Assessment

2. Engage in a 360-Degree Feedback Assessment

3. Improve How We Deliver Feedback

4. Know Why We Sometimes Act Out of Character and What To Do About It

5. Take Time for Self-Reflection

6. Ask for Informal Feedback

3 GOALS–SELF-AWARENESS

GOAL #1: _____

Why It Matters to Me: _____

Action Plan

Immediate: _____

Short-term (6-12 months): _____

Long-term (12 months-ongoing): _____

GOAL #2: _____

Why It Matters to Me: _____

Action Plan

Immediate: _____

Short-term (6-12 months): _____

Long-term (12 months-ongoing): _____

GOAL #3: _____

Why It Matters to Me: _____

Action Plan

Immediate: _____

Short-term (6-12 months): _____

Long-term (12 months-ongoing): _____

PILLAR 2: CIVILITY

Politeness and civility are the best capital ever invested in business. Large stores, gilt signs, flaming advertisements, will all prove unavailing if you or your employees treat your patrons abruptly.

—P. T. Barnum

Definition of Civility:

In general civility can be defined as "politeness and courtesy in behavior and speech." However, defining "incivility" gives a much better perception of what it means to be civil. According to Dr. Christine Pearson and Christine Porath, incivility is "the exchange of seemingly inconsequential inconsiderate words and deeds that violate conventional norms of workplace conduct."

Why Civility Matters:

Incivility can lead to:

1. Desire for Retribution
2. Impaired Performance
3. Lowered Team Spirit
4. Decreased Employee Engagement/Commitment
5. Poorer Physical Health

Putting Civility Into Action:

1. Say "Please" and "Thank You"
2. Create a Team Charter
3. Model Positive Behavior
4. Watch Your Language
5. Put Away Electronic Devices
6. Encourage Feelings of Psychological Safety
7. Take Immediate Corrective Action When Warranted

3 GOALS—CIVILITY

GOAL #1: _____

Why It Matters to Me: _____

Action Plan

Immediate: _____

Short-term (6-12 months): _____

Long-term (12 months-ongoing): _____

GOAL #2: _____

Why It Matters to Me: _____

Action Plan

Immediate: _____

Short-term (6-12 months): _____

Long-term (12 months-ongoing): _____

GOAL #3: _____

Why It Matters to Me: _____

Action Plan

Immediate: _____

Short-term (6-12 months): _____

Long-term (12 months-ongoing): _____

PILLAR 3: HUMILITY

Humility is the solid foundation of all virtues.

—Confucius

Definition of Humility:

Humility is recognizing that we do not have all the answers, and are willing to accept new perspectives "without feeling that the self has been obliterated or damaged."

Why Humility Matters:

1. Better Quality Decision-Making

2. Higher Employee Engagement

3. More Effective Leadership

Putting Humility Into Action:

1. Take Ownership of Your Mistakes

2. Be Open to Learning and Asking Questions

3. Shine the Spotlight on Your Team

3 GOALS—HUMILITY

GOAL #1: _____

Why It Matters to Me: _____

Action Plan

Immediate: _____

Short-term (6-12 months): _____

Long-term (12 months-ongoing): _____

GOAL #2: _____

Why It Matters to Me: _____

Action Plan

Immediate: _____

Short-term (6-12 months): _____

Long-term (12 months-ongoing): _____

GOAL #3: _____

Why It Matters to Me: _____

Action Plan

Immediate: _____

Short-term (6-12 months): _____

Long-term (12 months-ongoing): _____

PILLAR 4: FOCUSING ON THE POSITIVE

In order to carry a positive action one must develop here a positive vision.

—Dalai Lama

Definition of Focusing on the Positive:

Focusing on the positive is not about eliminating the negative altogether—it is about deciding where you are going to invest the majority of your time and attention.

Why Focusing on the Positive Matters:

1. Improved Physical Health

2. Greater Creativity

3. Positive Group Attitude (Emotional Contagion)

Putting Focusing on the Positive Into Action:

1. When Giving Praise, Make it Descriptive Rather Than Evaluative

2. See the Opportunity in Failure

3. Focus on Strengths

3 GOALS—FOCUSING ON THE POSITIVE

GOAL #1: _____

Why It Matters to Me: _____

Action Plan

Immediate: _____

Short-term (6-12 months): _____

Long-term (12 months-ongoing): _____

GOAL #2: _____

Why It Matters to Me: _____

Action Plan

Immediate: _____

Short-term (6-12 months): _____

Long-term (12 months-ongoing): _____

GOAL #3: _____

Why It Matters to Me: _____

Action Plan

Immediate: _____

Short-term (6-12 months): _____

Long-term (12 months-ongoing): _____

PILLAR 5: MEANING AND PURPOSE

Life is never made unbearable by circumstances, but only by lack of meaning and purpose.

—Viktor Frankl

Definition of Meaning and Purpose:

Purpose is the reason something is done. Meaning comes from ascribing a greater value to that purpose. For instance, a car can have purpose (e.g., to drive from points A to B) and meaning (e.g., it was the first car your grandfather owned). When we value the purpose of a company (e.g., helping others), then its purpose has greater meaning to us.

Why Meaning and Purpose Matter:

1. Higher Job Satisfaction/Well-Being

2. Increased Engagement

3. Better Performance

4. Greater Motivation

Putting Meaning and Purpose Into Action:

1. Find Greater Meaning in Your Work

2. "Outsource Inspiration"

3. Create a Shared Sense of Purpose

4. Identify Personal Core Values

5. Have More Meaningful Discussions With Your Employees

6. Spend Time Engaged in Meaningful Activities

3 GOALS—MEANING AND PURPOSE

GOAL #1: _____

Why It Matters to Me: _____

Action Plan

Immediate: _____

Short-term (6-12 months): _____

Long-term (12 months-ongoing): _____

GOAL #2: _____

Why It Matters to Me: _____

Action Plan

Immediate: _____

Short-term (6-12 months): _____

Long-term (12 months-ongoing): _____

GOAL #3: _____

Why It Matters to Me: _____

Action Plan

Immediate: _____

Short-term (6-12 months): _____

Long-term (12 months-ongoing): _____

PILLAR 6: EMPATHY

Empathy is about standing in someone else's shoes, feeling with his or her heart, seeing with his or her eyes. Not only is empathy hard to outsource and automate, but it makes the world a better place.

—**Daniel Pink**

Definition of Empathy:

Empathy is being aware of the thoughts, feelings, and experiences of others without necessarily walking in their shoes.

Why Empathy Matters:

1. Superior Performance

2. Effective Leadership

3. Better Bottom Line

Putting Empathy Into Action:

1. Stop Focusing on Yourself

2. Visit the Front Lines

3. AMPPlify Your Listening

4. Break the Golden Rule

5. Incorporate "Capacity for Empathy" into Hiring and Promotions

3 GOALS—EMPATHY

GOAL #1: _____

Why It Matters to Me: _____

Action Plan

Immediate: _____

Short-term (6-12 months): _____

Long-term (12 months-ongoing): _____

GOAL #2: _____

Why It Matters to Me: _____

Action Plan

Immediate: _____

Short-term (6-12 months): _____

Long-term (12 months-ongoing): _____

GOAL #3: _____

Why It Matters to Me: _____

Action Plan

Immediate: _____

Short-term (6-12 months): _____

Long-term (12 months-ongoing): _____

APPENDIX

PILLAR 1: SELF-AWARENESS

Hogan Assessment Scales

HPI Primary Scales*:

Adjustment

- Low scorers tend to be open to feedback, candid and honest, moody and self-critical.

- High scorers tend to be calm, steady under pressure, and resistant to feedback.

Ambition

- Low scorers tend to be good team players, willing to let others lead, and complacent.

- High scorers tend to be energetic, competitive, restless, and forceful.

Sociability

- Low scorers tend to be good at working alone, quiet, and socially reactive.

- High scorers tend to be outgoing, talkative, and attention-seeking.

Interpersonal Sensitivity

- Low scorers tend to be direct and frank, willing to confront others, cold, and tough.

- High scorers tend to be friendly, warm, and conflict averse.

Prudence

- Low scorers tend to be flexible, open-minded, and impulsive.

- High scorers tend to be organized, dependable, and inflexible.

Inquisitive

- Low scorers tend to be practical, not easily bored, and uninventive.

- High scorers tend to be imaginative, quick-witted, and poor implementers.

Learning Approach

- Low scorers tend to be hands-on learners, focused on their interests, and technology averse.

- High scorers tend to be interested in learning, insightful, and intolerant of the less-informed.

HDS Dark Side Scales*:

Excitable

- Low scorers seem calm to the point of appearing to lack passion or urgency.

- High scorers display dramatic emotional peaks and valleys regarding people and projects.

Skeptical

- Low scorers seem trusting to the point of naivety.

- High scorers are negative or cynical and expect to be betrayed.

Cautious

- Low scorers are willing to take risks without adequate risk assessment.

- High scorers are reluctant to take risks regardless of risk assessment.

Reserved

- Low scorers are too concerned about the feelings of others.

- High scorers are indifferent to the feelings of others.

Leisurely

- Low scorers appear to lack an agenda or direction.

- High scorers are passive-aggressive and agenda-driven.

Bold

- Low scorers appear to lack self-confidence and resolve.

- High scorers seem assertive, self-promoting, and overly self-confident.

Mischievous

- Low scorers are conservative, compliant, and unadventurous.

- High scorers are impulsive, limit-testing, and devious at times.

Colorful

- Low scorers are modest, unassuming, quiet, and self-restrained.

- High scorers are attention-seeking, dramatic, and socially prominent.

Imaginative

- Low scorers are practical, rely on routine, and often lack new ideas.

- High scorers may seem impractical, unpredictable, and offer unusual ideas.

Diligent

- Low scorers have poor attention to detail and tend to over-delegate.

- High scorers are picky, overly conscientious, and tend to micromanage.

Dutiful

- Low scorers are overly independent and seem to resent authority.

- High scorers are excessively eager to please superiors.

MVPI Scales*:

Recognition

- Low scorers prefer to share credit and avoid calling attention to themselves.

- High scorers value public acknowledgement and prefer high-visibility projects.

Power

- Low scorers prefer to let other people lead and avoid confrontation and competition.

- High scorers value leadership positions and prefer opportunities to get ahead.

Hedonism

- Low scorers value business-like and professional settings, preferring serious and formal work environments.

- High scorers value colorful and entertaining environments, including fun and open-minded settings.

Altruistic

- Low scorers place more value on their own work and prefer productivity over morale.

- High scorers value helping other people and prefer customer-focused environments.

Affiliation

- Low scorers prefer working alone or in isolation, valuing independence.

- High scorers prefer working with others or on teams, valuing social interaction.

Tradition

- Low scorers prefer flexibility and autonomy, valuing challenging established procedures.

- High scorers prefer the status quo and avoid people that do not share beliefs.

Security

- Low scorers value risk taking and experimentation, preferring adventurous settings.

- High scorers prefer consistency and predictability, avoiding taking unnecessary risks.

Commerce
- Low scorers value relationships over profitability and are less concerned about financial issues.

- High scorers prefer environments that focus on the bottom line and value activities related to financial matters.

Aesthetics
- Low scorers value practicality over appearance and prefer routines and repetition.

- High scorers value innovation and creativity, preferring individual style and appearance.

Science
- Low scorers prefer people over technology and value intuition and experience.

- High scorers value analysis and problem solving, preferring to work with data and objective facts.

Scale descriptions from Hogan Assessments product descriptions. For more information about the Hogan Assessment, visit www.hoganassessments.com.

TAIS Psychological Factors

Attentional Factors:

- **Awareness** - One's environmental sensitivity and ability to react to external stimuli.

- **External Distractibility** - How easily one is distracted by irrelevant tasks.

- **Analysis/Conceptual** - Ability to problem solve.

- **Internal Distractibility** - How easily one is distracted by thoughts/feelings.

- **Action/Focused** - Attention to detail and tolerance for engaging in repetitive behavior.

- **Reduced Flexibility** - How easily one can shift their focus.

Interpersonal Factors:

- **Information Processing** - How one handles change, shifting priorities, and lack of structure.

- **Orientation Toward Rules and Risks** - How easily one thinks outside of the box and bends the rules.

- **Control** - The need to take on a leadership role.

- **Self-Confidence** - One's sense of self-worth in different performance settings.

- **Physical Competitiveness** - How much one enjoys competition.

- **Decision-Making Style** - Tendency to obsess and/or overanalyze a situation before making a decision.

- **Extroversion** - One's need to be with others.

- **Introversion** - One's need to work alone.

- **Expression of Ideas** - How comfortable one is with expressing ideas and having them challenged.

- **Expression of Criticism and Anger** - How easily one expresses anger/frustration and challenges others.

- **Expression of Support and Affection** - How easily one expresses positivity and support of others.

- **Self-Critical** - One's level of self-doubt.

- **Focus Over Time** - How easily one makes long-term sacrifices to accomplish goals.

- **Performance Under Pressure** - One's comfort with taking a leadership role in high-pressure situations.

PILLAR 6: EMPATHY

Management Research Group's Leadership Effectiveness Analysis (LEA 360) Six Core Leadership Functions and Twenty-Two Behavioral Leadership Practices*

Creating a Vision

- Conservative: Studying problems in light of past practices to ensure predictability, reinforce the status quo, and minimize risk.

- Innovative: Feeling comfortable in fast-changing environments; being willing to take risks and to consider new and untested approaches.

- Technical: Acquiring and maintaining in-depth knowledge in your field or area of focus; using your expertise and specialized knowledge to study issues in depth and draw conclusions.

- Self: Emphasizing the importance of making decisions independently; looking to yourself as the prime vehicle for decision-making.

- Strategic: Taking a long-range, broad approach to problem solving and decision-making through objective analysis, thinking ahead, and planning.

Developing Followership

- Persuasive: Building commitment by convincing others and winning them over to your point of view.

- Outgoing: Acting in an extroverted, friendly, and informal manner; showing a capacity to quickly establish free and easy interpersonal relationships.

- Excitement: Operating with a good deal of energy, intensity, and emotional expression; having a capacity for keeping others enthusiastic and involved.

- Restraint: Maintaining a low-key, understated, and quiet interpersonal demeanor by working to control your emotional expression.

Implementing the Vision

- Structuring: Adopting a systematic and organized approach; preferring to work in a precise, methodical manner; developing and utilizing guidelines and procedures.

- Tactical: Emphasizing the production of immediate results by focusing on short-range, hands-on, practical strategies.

- Communication: Stating clearly what you want and expect from others; clearly expressing your thoughts and ideas; maintaining a precise and constant flow of information.

- Delegation: Enlisting the talents of others to help meet objectives by giving them important activities and sufficient autonomy to exercise their own judgment.

Following Through

- Control: Adopting an approach in which you take nothing for granted, set deadlines for certain actions and are persistent in monitoring the progress of activities to ensure that they are completed on schedule.

- Feedback: Letting others know in a straightforward manner what you think of them, how well they have performed and if they have met your needs and expectations.

Achieving Results

- Management Focus: Seeking to exert influence by being in positions of authority, taking charge, and leading and directing the efforts of others.

- Dominant: Pushing vigorously to achieve results through an approach which is forceful, assertive and competitive.

- Production: Adopting a strong orientation toward achievement; holding high expectations for yourself and others; pushing yourself and others to achieve at high levels.

Team Playing

- Cooperation: Accommodating the needs and interests of others by being willing to defer performance on your own objectives in order to assist colleagues with theirs.

- Consensual: Valuing the ideas and opinions of others and collecting their input as part of your decision-making process.

- Authority: Showing loyalty to the organization; respecting the ideas and opinions of people in authority and using them as resources for information, direction, and decisions.

- Empathy: Demonstrating an active concern for people and their needs by forming close and supportive relationships with others.

Definitions of functions as described in MRG's LEA Sample Report found at: https://www.mrg.com/wp-content/uploads/2018/04/LEA-Sample-Report.pdf.

ABOUT THE AUTHOR

Craig Dowden, PhD is president of Craig Dowden & Associates (www.craigdowden.com), a firm focused on supporting clients in achieving leadership and organizational excellence by leveraging the science of peak performance. Craig is a highly-respected executive coach and award-winning international keynote speaker.

Craig is also the Chief Leadership Officer (CLO) of Keynote Search (keynotesearch.com), an award-winning firm that helps organizations to Find, Fit, and Retain business-critical talent. Backed by leading AI technology, codified processes, dedicated coaching, and onboarding support, Keynote Search maximizes the potential success of your next hire.

Dowden and his team prides themselves in providing world-class content, which is why he is passionate about sharing the latest research on positive leadership and peak performance with his clients to maximize their individual and collective success.

To date, he has interviewed over sixty CEOs of top North American companies, including McDonald's, IKEA, and VIA Rail. He has also interviewed widely known bestselling authors and TED speakers, including Marshall Goldsmith, Daniel Pink, Adam Grant, Susan Cain, Barry Schwartz, Marilee Adams, Adam Bryant, and Doug Stone. He routinely integrates these conversations and insights into his client work.

You can connect with him by email (craig@craigdowden.com), LinkedIn, or follow him on Twitter @craigdowden.

A Special Offer from ForbesBooks

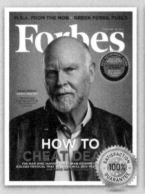  

Other publications bring you business news. Subscribing to *Forbes* magazine brings you business knowledge and inspiration you can use to make your mark.

- Insights into important business, financial and social trends
- Profiles of companies and people transforming the business world
- Analysis of game-changing sectors like energy, technology and health care
- Strategies of high-performing entrepreneurs

Your future is in our pages.

To see your discount and subscribe go to Forbesmagazine.com/bookoffer.

Forbes